RHS

GREENER GARDENING

Containers

RHS

GREENER GARDENING

Containers

The Sustainable Guide to Growing Flowers, Shrubs and Crops in Pots

Ann Treneman

MITCHELL BEAZLEY

RHS Greener Gardening: Containers
Author: Ann Treneman
First published in Great Britain in 2024
by Mitchell Beazley, an imprint of Octopus Publishing Group Ltd,
Carmelite House, 50 Victoria Embankment, London EC4Y 0DZ

www.octopusbooks.co.uk
An Hachette UK Company
www.hachette.co.uk

Published in association with the
Royal Horticultural Society
© 2024 Quarto Publishing plc

ISBN: 978-1-78472-931-8

A CIP record of this book is available from the British Library

Printed and bound in China

Mitchell Beazley Publisher: Alison Starling
Mitchell Beazley Editorial Assistant: Ellen Sleath
RHS Book Publishing Manager: Helen Griffin
RHS Consultant Editor: Simon Maughan
RHS Head of Editorial: Tom Howard

Conceived, designed and produced by
The Bright Press,
an imprint of The Quarto Group.
1 Triptych Place, London, SE1 9SH
(0)20 7700 9000
www.Quarto.com

Publisher: James Evans
Art Director: James Lawrence
Editorial Director: Isheeta Mustafi/Anna Southgate
Managing Editor: Jacqui Sayers
Editor: Emily Angus
Project Editor: Rica Dearman
Design: Clare Barber/Studio Noel
Illustrations: Sarah Skeate
Picture Researchers: Tom Broadbent/Katie Greenwood/Emily Angus

The Royal Horticultural Society is the UK's leading gardening charity dedicated to advancing horticulture and promoting good gardening. Its charitable work includes providing expert advice and information in print, online and at its five major gardens and annual shows, training gardeners of every age, creating hands-on opportunities for children to grow plants and sharing research into plants, wildlife, wellbeing and environmental issues affecting gardeners.

For more information visit www.rhs.org.uk
or call 020 3176 5800.

MIX
Paper | Supporting
responsible forestry
FSC® C016973

Contents

Introduction 8

PART 1

Setting up your container garden 10

Choosing where to site your containers 12

Choosing the right containers for your garden 16

Equipment: what you'll need 20

PART 2

Greener container gardening techniques 22

Sourcing plants for your containers 24

Containers and contents 28

How to make natural plant supports 36

Circular supports 38

Tepee supports 39

Watering your container plants 40

Self-watering (wicking bed) 44

Feeding your plants 46

Working with nature 50

Plant annoyances and diseases 52

Staying on track 54

PART 3

Creating a container garden 56

Growing in groups 58

Ecosystems and habitats in a pot 60

Choosing a theme 62

Creating a plan for your container garden 66

Get creative 68

Creating eco habitats 70

Setting up a container pocket forest 74

Hazel and sorbus pocket forest 76

Putting together a patio orchard 78

Eco-friendly patio orchard 80

Creating a flowery meadow in a pot 82

Mini meadow 84

Establishing a nectar café 86

Welcome to the 'nectar bar' 88

Wild edibles in pots 90

Setting up a potager pot plot 92

Planting a potager plot 94

Constructing crazy containers 96

Winter wonder 98

Dry crevice garden   100

Stone trough crevice garden   102

Setting up a rain garden   104

Pond in a pot   106

Garden in a metal trough   108

Weeds on show   110

PART 4

Plants to grow   112

Tree profiles   114

Edimental profiles   118

Shrub profiles   124

Perennial profiles   128

Annual profiles   132

Shade lover profiles   136

Grass profiles   140

Bulb profiles   144

Aquatic profiles   148

Dry garden plant profiles   152

Herb profiles   156

Climber profiles   160

Wild weed profiles   164

Charts and planners   168

Further reading   170

Index   171

Picture credits   176

Introduction

This is the book that I wish I'd had when I started to create container gardens. I always wanted to garden in a greener way, but at times my rather haphazard gardening choices – often made on the spur of the moment – were part of the problem, not the solution. Gradually, though, I began to adjust my way of thinking and to make decisions that benefitted not only my plants, but also the environment and wildlife.

GO GREENER

Your first thought when setting up your new container garden should be 'What do I already have that I can use?'

There is something thrilling when you can see that a few pots on the patio are so much more than a spot of colour. Plants and containers, when grouped together, interact with each other, creating their own mini ecosystem that also attracts wildlife. You can enhance this natural process by making eco-friendly decisions, some of them simple, from the get-go.

Here is a practical guide on how to make greener choices when it comes to materials, design, plant choice and maintenance. It embraces the philosophy of reduce, reuse and recycle and shows how to choose plants and combinations that bring wildlife into your garden. Containers bring joy on many levels – with their combinations of plant size, colour, texture and shape – but attracting wildlife adds

another dimension. It is especially satisfying to sit back and watch as your pots become a nectar pitstop for bees and butterflies. I still can't get over how, just a few days after creating my small container pond, a stunning blue dragonfly came to visit (and not just once).

It is one of my mantras that greener gardening does not mean that you have to settle for less when it comes to beauty or impact. This book aims to inspire with a series of container themes that range from the large, as in a pocket forest or patio orchard, to something as small as a 'nectar café' window box. At its heart is the belief that anyone, anywhere, can create a garden, no matter what size, that will benefit the planet. Gardening is for everyone, and the greener, the better.

Setting up your container garden

Creating a container garden can be like putting together a real-life photosynthesizing jigsaw puzzle. One of the joys of developing such a garden is that you have so much scope for choice, and this chapter will guide you through how to make the all-important initial decisions in a sustainable and wildlife-friendly way. Firstly, what is the right location for your new garden? And what material – and size – will you choose for the containers themselves? Then, of course, you'll need to acquire the right equipment for the job. As Alexander Graham Bell, who loved gardening as well as inventing, said: 'Before anything else, preparation is the key to success.'

Choosing where to site your containers

There are no absolute rules for finding the right location for your containers except this one: thoughtful assessment is the key to success. You won't go wrong if you start out by taking the maxim of 'right plant, right place' as your guide. Small or large, urban or rural, finding the right place is absolutely key.

When setting up your container garden, think 'location, location, location', but with a twist – see the site from a plant's point of view. You may have chosen a spot because you'd like to sit there but, first of all, find out what it will be like for your plants.

Sun and shade, aspect and exposure are all factors to take into consideration. Having done that, you may then need to calibrate your plant choices. After all, if you fancy a fernery, those fronds will never be fond of a baking-hot patio corner!

Group plants that prefer the same conditions together in one spot.

Which way does your garden face?

The direction your garden faces will have a huge impact on how much sun it receives at different times of the day. Before you start to position any containers, stand outside with your back to the house and use a compass to show which way you (and your garden) are facing. Using the diagrams below as a guide (these illustrations show light and shade patterns in the northern hemisphere), you can work out how much direct sunlight your garden will receive. Other things to consider are how much shade might be thrown by trees outside of your plot, or any tall buildings nearby.

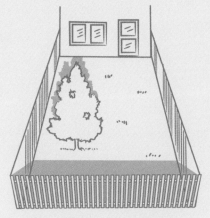

South-facing gardens will receive
the most sunlight.

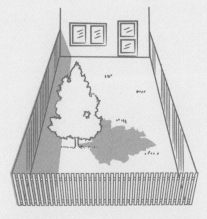

West-facing gardens will have afternoon
and early-evening light.

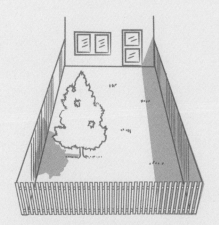

East-facing gardens
will have more morning light.

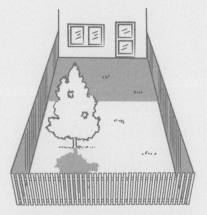

North-facing gardens will receive
the least light.

Sun and shade

Aspect isn't everything, of course. Just because your container garden is south-facing doesn't necessarily mean it will receive nonstop sun. Are there trees nearby that will place it in the shade for part of the day? Or will it be affected by a shed or a wall? It's worth taking the time to check out the amount of sunlight (or shade) at various times throughout a day.

This is crucial to its success, because the amount of sunlight available will determine which plants will thrive in the spot. Sunny spots mean the plants will be thirstier and require more watering – especially in the summer – while shady spots can be made more light-reflective by using techniques such as painting a wall white or using mirrors.

Wind and rain

How exposed is your spot? If your containers are on a balcony or windowsills, then you will need to be aware of the wind factor. This is also the case for some locations in an 'on-the-ground' garden – any place that is high or not secluded can be susceptible to wind. It is also important to find out if your spot is in a 'rain shadow', as many porches and patios are partially covered.

Being in a rain shadow means that the wind can dry out and cause 'wind scorch' on leaves, and containers in these places will need more watering. You could reduce these effects by shielding windy spots with adjacent 'screen' planting, or moving the containers even a short distance so that they will receive more rain.

GO GREENER

All containers will need watering, so think 'rainwater' from the start. Are there water butts nearby? If not, can you install one?

Any available light in this shady courtyard is enhanced by the white walls and pale flooring.

TIP

You can always garden 'up' by grouping plants on ladders or creating shelves on a wall to increase the number of plants you can fit in your space.

What's in the neighbourhood?

Step back and have a look at what is adjacent to or near the spot you have chosen.

Will your plants be the only greenery in the area? If so, for maximum wellbeing benefits, you will want more than one container. What kind of wildlife lives nearby already? Is there an adjacent border or trellis with plants that already attract some bees and other insects? Is there a pond nearby? Are there any pets – or even unwelcome guests (as some think of foxes and/or grey squirrels, because they often like to dig into containers and you'll need to set up some physical defences) – that need to be taken into consideration?

An unloved spot may be fitting

Not all locations are immediately obvious. Containers can be placed on the ground, on walls or arbours, either fixed or hanging from hooks. A well-placed container garden can add greenery and colour to the most unlikely places, including next to bike and bin sheds. Feeling the heat in the city? Container climbers up a wall can help regulate the temperature inside. Look at your entire outdoor space, including that dark passageway or tiny front garden mostly used as a car parking space. Could containers enhance these unloved spaces? Choose low-maintenance plants in places that are not close to water and foot access.

Choosing the right containers for your garden

There's a huge range of containers out there, from the traditional variety in garden centres to a host of recycled objects just waiting to be found in salvage yards. You can also make your own or repurpose some old walking boots.

Natural materials include terracotta, stone and wood; the only plastic in your garden should be by reusing whatever plastic you may already have – avoid buying it new, as there are already some 500 million plastic plant pots in circulation, and only a third will ever be recycled. Think natural, local, reusable.

You may be tempted to choose your containers on looks alone, but think about these practical considerations: larger containers mean less watering and more room to accommodate a variety of plants. Also, grouping together several containers of varying sizes and heights will create a mini ecosystem and that benefits wildlife, too. Larger pots also allow for more efficient watering and reduced fluctuation of moisture and temperature in the compost.

GO GREENER

When buying containers, remember that saucers and reservoirs mean that water can be caught and easily retained.

Sourcing and decorating

Get salvaging Visit your local reclamation yard for inspiration such as old chimney stacks, birdcages, metal wheelbarrows, old kettles or teapots, boots or wellies, used tyres and old birdhouses.

Get creative Add your own personal touches to containers with environmentally friendly paint, tiles or other decorative items. Or why not trim a planting box with small, white birch branches?

TIP

When it comes to containers, allow room for a variety of plants (and wildlife); aim for ones with a diameter of at least 48cm (19in).

Types of container

◐ **Terracotta pots** Used since ancient times, these are made of fired clay and are porous, which helps prevent root rot and/or soil disease. They are heavy, which makes them stable but also means you won't want to move them too often. The glazed varieties can be frost-proof, but check the claims on the label carefully.

◑ **Alpine hypertufa troughs** These rough-looking troughs look great with alpines and even manage to be relatively lightweight. They are a good DIY project (you can make a trough using something as basic as cardboard boxes) – but avoid the traditional recipe, which includes cement, peat moss and perlite. Greener versions are made with coir and applied to old sinks, recycled fish and vegetable boxes. Sustainable alternatives to cement are harder to find, but include lime which, for instance, can be mixed with hemp hurd to make hempcrete.

More types of container

◉ **Intermediate Bulk Containers (IBCs)**
These recycled industrial containers are readily available, modular and customizable. Many come in metal 'cages', which allows for hanging plant options. They will suit larger planting schemes that include trees.

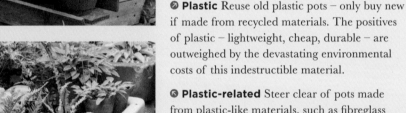

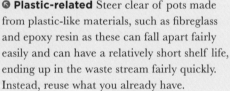

❷ **Plastic** Reuse old plastic pots – only buy new if made from recycled materials. The positives of plastic – lightweight, cheap, durable – are outweighed by the devastating environmental costs of this indestructible material.

◈ **Plastic-related** Steer clear of pots made from plastic-like materials, such as fibreglass and epoxy resin as these can fall apart fairly easily and can have a relatively short shelf life, ending up in the waste stream fairly quickly. Instead, reuse what you already have.

◕ **Ceramic sink** These can look great filled with alpines.

◔ **Wood** Crates, barrels and boxes made from sustainable wood (look for the FSC logo when buying new) are naturally attractive – but avoid softwoods that have been preserved with toxic chemicals or heat treated. Instead, use durable timber, such as western red cedar or green oak, which looks great and will last for years. Alternatively, treat plain softwood with an eco-friendly preservative such as linseed oil.

● **Stone** Cast stone planters are reliable in all weather and provide some insulation for your plants. They come in many shapes and sizes, including old stone troughs. Be warned, however: they can be extremely heavy to lift, so do use pot trolleys to safely lift big containers.

● **Metal** Buy new or – even better – reuse an old metal bathtub, water tank or, if you are thinking big, a farm water trough. Options include stainless and galvanized steel, zinc, tin, copper and cast iron. Metal holds water well but there is virtually no insulation, so it will heat up in the sun and get cold in the winter. Insulate the sides below the soil line with newspaper or cardboard.

● **Fabric** Make these soft and pliable 'pots' from recycled materials (including plastic) mixed with fabric weaves (options include hemp and felt). They are porous, which allows roots to breathe. Many are reusable, but some will not be long-lasting and will need replacing.

● **Vertical structures, hanging baskets and 'living' walls** You will need lightweight containers for vertical spaces (such as placing plants on a ladder or wall). You could use birdcages and even household 'junk', such as old colanders, for hanging baskets.

ECO WORRIER

When choosing containers, take into consideration their transport miles, which add to their carbon footprints.

Equipment: what you'll need

What tools you require depend, to some extent, on the size of your containers. For instance, you may want more than a small hand trowel if you are planting a tree. Think quality, not quantity. Cheap, imported tools are not as eco-friendly as locally produced ones; good-quality ones can last a lifetime. Avoid plastic and go for those that use sustainable wood.

Tools

Hand trowel and fork These come in varying sizes and shapes. For larger containers, a mid-sized handle will offer you more flexibility when planting, especially for hard-to-reach areas. Look for rust-resistant stainless steel with FSC wooden handles.

Transplanting trowel These are not essential but are handy, especially when planting lots of bulbs. They are narrower than the usual trowel, and measurement markings on the blade make it easy to plant at the right depth.

Secateurs Essential for pruning, deadheading, cutting back and harvesting. There are two main types: bypass secateurs have two blades which cut like a pair of scissors – they are ideal for smaller stems as well as greener growth; anvil secateurs have one blade that cuts down onto a flat surface – these are good for thicker, woodier stems. Keep both sharp to ensure clean cutting.

Sharpening stone Regular use will avoid blunt tools. Whetstones are fine-grained stone and will need either oil or water for lubrication. Diamond-coated blocks or portable pocket-sized sharpeners work well for secateurs and are also suitable for spades and hoes.

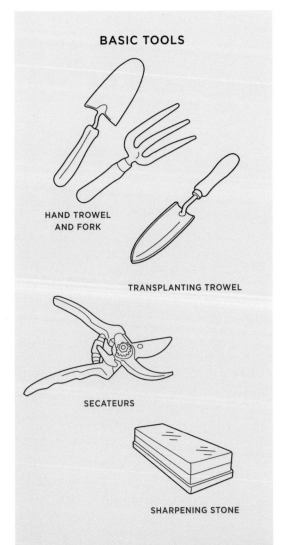

BASIC TOOLS

HAND TROWEL
AND FORK

TRANSPLANTING TROWEL

SECATEURS

SHARPENING STONE

ADDITIONAL TOOLS

WATERING CAN

GARDEN TWINE

TRUG

GLOVES

DUSTPAN
AND BRUSH

KNEELING PAD

NOTEBOOK

MEASURING TAPE
OR RULER

Other essentials

Watering can Choose a metal one and a size that works for you and fits with the size of your containers – and remember that the cans will be much heavier when filled. A fine rose works for young plants and, as plants grow, a spout will make it easier to target the base of the plant. A long spout is best for watering larger containers.

Garden twine Many natural materials, such as jute, sisal, cotton and wool can be made into twine, but hemp twine is arguably the best from a sustainable point of view. It is strong, biodegradable and compostable, as well as being a sustainable crop.

Basket or trug These are handy for carrying just about anything you need and look great in traditional wood or wicker.

Gloves Look for lightweight gloves in cotton with FSC natural rubber.

Dustpan and brush Most are plastic, so search out those that are 100 per cent recycled or long-lasting wood and steel pans.

Kneeling pad Especially handy if you are working on a hard surface such as a patio. Look for waxed cotton and canvas. Avoid polyester.

Design aids

Notebook Collect your designs and drawings in a garden notebook; you can also note down planting and flowering dates each year.

Measuring tape or ruler Go for a metal ruler or other plastic-free varieties.

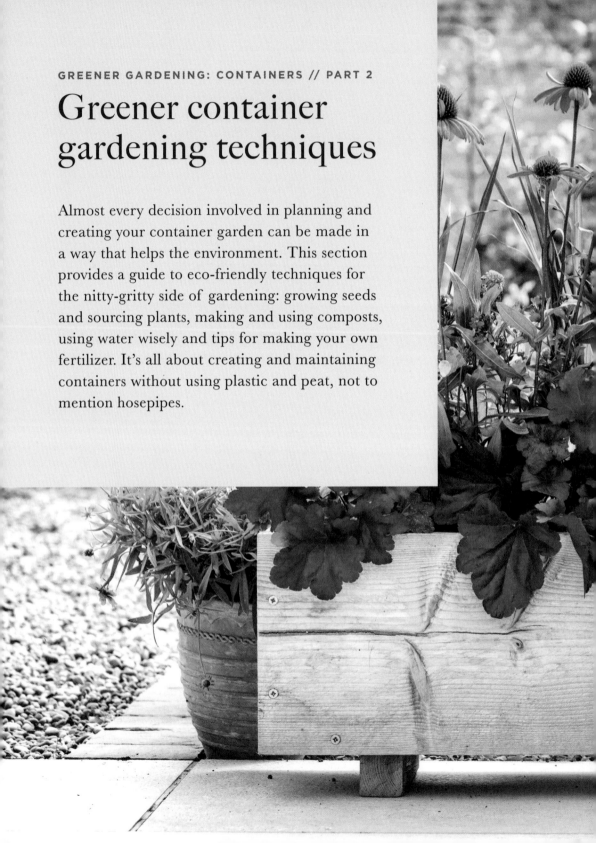

Greener container gardening techniques

Almost every decision involved in planning and creating your container garden can be made in a way that helps the environment. This section provides a guide to eco-friendly techniques for the nitty-gritty side of gardening: growing seeds and sourcing plants, making and using composts, using water wisely and tips for making your own fertilizer. It's all about creating and maintaining containers without using plastic and peat, not to mention hosepipes.

Sourcing plants for your containers

There are so many ways to grow or acquire the plants you need.
A lot depends on your planting plan, of course – annuals are
often best grown from seed and many perennials can be easily
propagated. And don't forget the free factor: explore local seed
and plant swap options and ask friends and neighbours for cuttings
or leftovers. If you decide to buy, then be on the alert as to plant
health and look out for those grown locally.

TIP

Some of the easiest
flowers to grow from seed
are annuals, including
poppies, cornflowers,
marigolds, sweet peas,
nasturtiums
and sunflowers.

Start with seeds

Seeds are a cost-effective and satisfying way to begin and your plants can be started off in recycled containers on your kitchen windowsill.

For easy biodegradable seed-growing containers, use egg cartons, recycled juice or yoghurt pots, toilet rolls cut in half, folded newspaper or buy coir plugs. (Don't forget to create drainage holes where necessary!)

Find seeds through swap or volunteer clubs and follow the directions on the packet for when and how to sow. Use peat-free potting compost and, if possible, water with captured rainwater, as plants prefer it without the additions found in tap water.

Once the first pair of 'true' leaves appears, give your seedling a feed with liquid seaweed or cold, stewed black tea, to give positive results for seedlings.

Plants grown inside will need to be transferred outside – but wait until they have three or four 'true' leaves and, initially, place them in a sheltered spot. Many annuals can be sown outside, directly into your containers, but check hardiness ratings to avoid disappointment after a cold spring night.

How to make a newspaper seed pot

1. Use two sheets of newspaper, folded lengthwise.

2. Wrap around a small jar with extra paper extended on the mouth side of the jar.

3. Stuff the extra paper into the jar mouth.

4. Remove the jar and then, turning it over, reinsert it with the bottom of the jar pressing down on the extra paper.

5. Press the jar down and then remove. The paper will now be in a 'pot' shape.

6. Tie string or twine around the 'pot' if required.

7. Fill with seed compost and get planting.

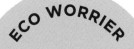

ECO WORRIER

Raise plants from seeds where possible or buy plug plants that have been grown locally without the use of peat.

Perennials

Many perennials can be propagated by division or cuttings but they need to be done in the autumn. These methods produce clones, which means you will know exactly what your new plant will look like when it's grown.

- The easiest form of propagation is division. In late autumn or early spring, use a spade to divide the roots, and replant directly into the container. It should flower that season.

- Root cuttings are best taken in autumn or winter when the plant is dormant. This is a good way to propagate Oriental poppies and verbascums.

- Tender perennials can be propagated by softwood cuttings taken in spring or semi-ripe cuttings in summer. Both are taken from new growth.

- For cuttings compost, use peat-free multipurpose potting compost and gritty sand.

Look out for perennials in pots that have congested roots. They can be easily split to make new plants.

Greener aeration options for your compost

Rather than use perlite or vermiculite, which are energy intensive in their manufacture, use other more sustainable materials such as fine bark chips, coarse wood fibres, sand or grit. Rice hulls also add porosity to compost, if you can find them. Crushed seashells are only good for very alkaline-loving plants.

BARK CHIPS

RICE HULLS

CRUSHED SEASHELLS

Buying plants

Think local and green in every way, and invest in plants with long-lasting appeal. Look for places that are embracing environmentally friendly practices, such as buying plants from local nurseries and going peat free.

Look for farmers markets and roadside plant stands (be sure that what is on offer is actually local), although mail order can be the only way to source hard-to-find plants. Look for bare-root plants, usually available from autumn to early spring, which come with very little packaging and are often cheaper.

Buy plants that are not in flower but have lots of buds, and turn the pots over to make sure they aren't pot-bound and check for disease. Avoid plastic pots and plants grown in peat compost.

Bigger does not equal better – often, several smaller plants set in a group will look more effective.

Getting plants for nothing

Look out for local seed and plant swaps, which are a great way to acquire plants as well as meet like-minded people. There are national networks as well as local community groups.

Local plant and seed swaps are often attached to community garden or botanical 'friend' groups. You can also browse 'seedy' and 'free-for-all' websites.

If you volunteer in a local school or community garden, you will often be rewarded with free cuttings or plants. Alternatively, ask friends if you can have a cutting from their plants.

Plants can self-seed, so don't make beds or containers overly neat and tidy. Give tiny plants a chance to grow. And note that some market-bought vegetables establish roots easily and can be grown on as a crop or just for fun.

Be on the lookout for community seed swaps or libraries: it's a great way to meet like-minded gardeners as well as explore new seed options.

Containers and contents

This is where you start to get your hands dirty – in a good way. What you fill your containers with is called compost, something of an all-purpose term for what is more accurately called 'growing media' or potting compost. Garden compost refers to the stuff made on a compost heap, useful as a soil-additive. For greener gardening, peat-free composts are the way forward.

Make your own compost

If making your own growing medium add (no more than 20 per cent by volume of), leaf mould bracken compost, bark chips, pine needles, grit, sand and so on. Don't overdo it though as very open potting media is a pain to keep moist and fertile. This will open up the porosity of the soil (see page 26), which is better for root growth.

TIP

To make your own soil-based compost, mix two parts sieved garden soil to one part garden compost.

Peat-free compost

Garden soil varies, but ideally is well structured with good drainage

It's checklist time

It's tempting to want to miss out a step or two, but your plants will thank you for sticking to these five essential rules – expanded on over the page – as it means they will get the very best environment in which to grow.

☐ Clean your containers.

☐ Examine containers for drainage holes and make more if necessary.

☐ To help with drainage, find 'crocks' (see right) to line the bottom of your pot. Crocks also prevent the loss of compost through drainage holes

☐ Choose a suitable growing medium or potting compost for the plants you want to grow (see page 30).

☐ Use mulch and soil improvers such as gravel and organic fertilizers (see page 34) to help create the right growing environment for your plants.

Clean

All containers need to be cleaned, even new ones. In those being reused, salts can build up in soils, leaving white deposits, which are unsightly but mostly harmless. Also remove moss or lichen, as well as make sure that there are no diseases lurking.

Use water with mild dish detergent or white distilled vinegar, and a stiff bristle brush wielded with a sense of purpose should do the trick. Wire brushes can be used but they will mark some containers. Rinse well and air dry.

Avoid bleach as it is, in every way, overkill.

Drainage

Drainage is essential in containers – there needs to be an adequate number of holes in the bottom. How many holes depends in part on what type of plants you will be growing – only a few plants, of the boggy variety, like being waterlogged. You don't want to create something akin to a colander, but one small hole in a large container will not be enough.

Space new holes several centimetres apart and use tape or a pencil to mark out where they will be. If you think a larger hole is needed, make a circle of holes near each other and tap with a hammer to collapse them together.

Using a drill works for most containers but, in some cases, a screwdriver and hammer or scissors could do the trick. If using a drill, use the correct drill bit: ceramic, masonry, metal or, for terracotta, diamond or masonry. Drill slowly. Haste really does make waste in this case.

When drilling terracotta, make sure the bottom of the pot is wet.

Crocks

You may need something to place at a tilt over the drainage holes to add to drainage and prevent soil seeping out. You could use broken-up pieces of terracotta, pottery, china or broken tiles. This practice is a great way of finding a way to reuse pots that are damaged beyond repair. Although this technique is largely outdated now, it does help retain soil and so it is largely a matter of personal choice for the gardener whether or not they continue to do use crocks in this manner.

Potting compost

There is a dizzying array of composts to choose from, but let your plants guide you and look for the one that is best for them. The word 'compost' has become something of an all-purpose term (see page 28). A more accurate term would be 'growing medium'.

Some composts are described as loam-based. This simply means that they contain a large component of soil, and they are often heavier as a result. Peat-free John Innes formulations are the ones to look for.

Look out for nutrients already added to the mix. This might be good for some plants, such as vegetables, but not so good for others. You can also improve the drainage of composts by adding grit. Most of the following below can be made as well as bought:

⊘ **Alpines/succulents** Free-draining mix of sand and soil

Annuals General mix or peat-free multipurpose compost

Aquatics Specialist aquatic compost or loam that is free from herbicides and fertilizers

⊘ **Fruit and vegetables** Nutrient-rich compost. Mix with added manure, or John Innes No.2

Herbs Compost or soil with added grit or sand

◐ **Lime-hating plants** Ericaceous compost

Perennial planting John Innes No.2 or John Innes seed compost

Seeds Low-nutrient finely graded compost

◑ **Wildflowers** Nutrient-poor soil with added grit

For peat's sake

The basic rule when buying any kind of growing media or soil is this: if the packaging doesn't say 'peat free', then it isn't. Peatlands are natural boggy areas that are the world's greatest carbon store on land. Any peat used in our gardens means carbon emissions have been released and habitats damaged. The UK government has said that peat in garden products will be banned but, for the time being, it will still be on sale.

What's in peat free Organic materials such as composted bark, coir or coconut fibre, green compost and inorganic rock-based materials such as sharp sand, rock wool and perlite.

Other things to consider Some of the ingredients of peat-free blends are not ideal in an eco-friendly world. For instance, coconut fibre may come from afar, while perlite is a non-renewable resource.

Speciality blends Many peat-free brands now have specialist composts for bulbs, potting, vegetables and even tomatoes.

Water retentive Look for ingredients such as wool, which will aid in water retention.

ECO WORRIER

Check for additives, such as water-retaining gels, which are are not organic, are of doubtful efficacy and are a potential source of plastic pollution.

31

Make your own garden compost

Homemade garden compost is very useful as a soil improver made from your garden and household waste, and the good news is that it's easy to create. And you won't need to have a big smelly pile – heaps and bins come in all sizes, including those for balconies. For all types, the basic idea remains the same: to break down a mix of 'green' matter and 'brown' or carbon-based material to create a dark brown substance with an almost spongy texture, full of nutrients.

TIP

If your compost bin or heap is attracting mice, then it is too dry. They won't stick around if you give it a good soaking and keep it the same consistency as a damp sponge.

Green
Grass cuttings, plants (avoid unwanted ones), fruit and vegetables

Brown
Twigs, branches, leaves, paper and cardboard

Mature
Garden compost ready to use

CREATING COMPOST

DO

- Set your bin in a spot with partial shade.

- Use green materials such as fruit and vegetable peelings, teabags, plant prunings (not diseased) and fresh grass cuttings.

- Use brown materials including cardboard, egg cartons, paper, fallen leaves and small twigs.

- Layer green and brown materials using 25–50% green.

- Make sure your compost doesn't dry out and add water if it does.

- Turn your pile or bin occasionally with a garden fork to keep things moving.

DON'T

- Add meat or dairy products to the mix (unless you have a 'digester').

- Add any diseased plants or include unwanted perennials.

- Use anything to do with poo – from dogs, cats or babies.

- Add lime or fertilizer as there is no need, despite the myth that it helps speed up the composting process.

- Be too impatient – it can take time and the 'cold' method will take at least six months, but the results are worth it.

GO GREENER

A bokashi bin uses fermentation to pickle food waste, including meat and dairy. It requires a special bacteria bran and fits in almost any space.

Hot or cold?

The two main differences between 'hot' and 'cold' methods are speed and effort.

The 'cold' method involves adding material piece by piece, so there is no opportunity for the compost to reach a good mass where heat is generated and retained.

With the 'hot' method, a lot of well-chosen and mixed ingredients are added in a short time in a sufficient volume so a hot ferment occurs.

Both hot and cold heaps or bins should be ventilated at the sides and the material within them turned at least once.

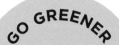

GO GREENER

Offcut branches, used to form the walls of your compost heap, are sustainable and allow for ventilation.

Other soil improvers

Gravel, grit or sand All promote drainage when mixed with soil or compost, however, adding too much to your potting compost can have the opposite effect and crush air spaces.

Manure This enriches and adds structure. Most types need six months to a year to rot down before they can be used. Rotting will also reduce the presence of pathogens harmful to human health.

Other natural soil improvers Bark chips and leaf mould can be mixed into the growing medium to help structure.

Mulch Adding a surface layer on top of your growing medium acts as a weed suppressant and a way to retain moisture. Use grit or gravel. Biodegradable mulches such as bark chips will slowly improve the soil as they rot down.

Maintenance

Once a year, usually in early spring, carry out a thorough inspection of your containers. Have the plants outgrown the container or has the container become too crowded? How long has it been since you refreshed the compost? Did any of the plants look peaky the year before? Do you need to inspect the roots or soil? Come up with a plan for the year ahead.

Even if not overcrowded, you need to refresh containers every two to four years by replacing a third of the growing medium. In years where you aren't refreshing, top-dress the container by removing 5cm (2in) of old growing medium from the top and replacing it with new.

In large containers the potting compost can become compacted over the years, so it may be worth removing it all and potting up again using fresh material.

Alternatively, rejuvenate what you already have, just so long as there are no diseases present or unwanted visitors. Remove old material, add 20 per cent bark chips to open up air spaces, and add some granular or powdered natural fertilizer.

Compost as you go

You can make a container version of the Hügelkultur (hill mound) method in which a planting pit is filled with logs and branches at the bottom with layers of 'green' matter, soil and then a straw mulch on top. Use the same scaled-down recipe for a container, which will need to be deep enough to make sure the roots are separated from the biodegrading green matter. Don't forget to use drainage holes and be ready for any counter-shrinkage.

How to pot up your containers

1. The best time to pot up your containers is in early spring, but leave tender perennials until late spring. Do winter containers in the autumn.

2. Assemble supplies including clean containers and an already mixed growing medium.

3. Water plants that you are going to pot up.

4. Place stones or crocks in the bottom of your container for extra drainage. Fill the container about four-fifths full of the growing medium.

5. Remove (well-watered) plants from their pots and arrange in their new 'home'.

6. Dig holes for each plant, adding more growing medium where necessary so that the top of the rootball is level with the surface.

7. Firm compost and add a layer of mulch.

8. Water the soil well.

How to make natural plant supports

Many plants will need support to look good, but there is no need to resort to canes, plastic string and/or netting. You could head to the salvage yard for the 'rusted steel' look in recycled and vintage items, but you can find a more natural look using materials in your garden. Natural plant supports are sustainable, blend in well and are, of course, free.

Plant supports are surprisingly easy to make. All you need for most are a pair of secateurs and the materials: branches and twigs or vines (or twine). If you don't have access to these materials in your garden, ask a friend, or contact a local park or allotment group. You can also buy them online or from a nursery.

The tree branches most used for supports are hazel, willow and birch, but for some supports – such as the tepee shape – you can use almost any pruned branches that are relatively straight.

Natural supports can be made in all shapes and sizes – there are the classic tepee or arches for climbers, knee-high circles for perennials and annuals, or even something as basic as twigs stuck into the ground to support garden peas.

A word of warning: if you use willow, then you may find that your support has suddenly burst into life itself, as willow tends to root easily.

If you have room in your garden, it is worth thinking about growing hazel and coppicing it for a regular supply of poles for tepees. The more flexible twiggy branches can be used to support smaller plants such as peas or lower climbers and scramblers.

ECO WORRIER

Use natural twine, such as hemp, jute, wool or sisal as they are biodegradable, unlike plastic string and netting.

Creative staking

Twist and turn The branches and twigs of twisted hazel are striking plant supports that are both sturdy and beautiful. They make a particular nice (and easy) cloche.

● **Branching out** The next time you prune a shrub or tree, save what you need so that you can make plant supports, as shown with these willow branches, for example, used here in a pot containing purple bell vine. The larger branches can be used to create a 'branch pile' in an out-of-the-way area of your garden. Wildlife (particularly insects) will love it.

TIP

Vines such as ivy or clematis can also be used to wrap and tie twigs together.

Circular supports

This circular support can be used for the likes of dahlias or any medium-sized perennial. The support should be about two-thirds the height of the eventual size of the plant.

Creating a circular support

1. Prune or harvest birch twigs and branches.

2. Trim them to about 1.5m (5ft), but make sure you have at least 30–40cm (12–16in) of thicker twig, with the rest being the easily pliable small birch twigs.

3. Push the thicker end into the soil in a circle around the plant.

4. At the top of the circle, weave the flexible twigs together (4A), with each branch leading on to the other until a full circle is formed (4B).

5. You can wrap twine around twigs to secure them if you think it necessary.

Variations on this support would include using branches as stakes in a circle and then using a vine such as pruned clematis to weave around the top of the stakes, creating a circle.

TIP

Build a structure that suits the style of your container planting, be it neat and tidy or wild and twisty.

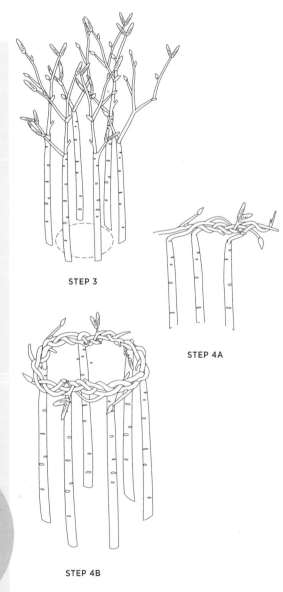

STEP 3

STEP 4A

STEP 4B

Tepee supports

Tepees are perfect for climbers. It's a sizeable structure and will be on display until the plant gets into full growth. You'll need some larger flexible branches as well as smaller flexible ones for the weaving.

Weaving a tepee support

1. Use straight, young flexible branches, such as one-year-old willow whips.

2. Cut them from the thicker end so they are all the same size you require, up to 2–3m (7–10ft).

3. While you can create a tepee with as few as three to five branches, it will be more secure if you use more (up to 10).

4. Fill a garden tub or large bucket with compost and push the branches down around the edge.

5. Tie the twigs together securely at the top using other twigs or twine.

6. About a fourth of the way up the tepee, start your first woven band. Weave the smaller flexible twigs around the circle of branches, going behind two branches and then in front of the third, repeating the pattern. When that twig ends, poke another one in to continue.

7. When you start the next circle, start your first 'two behind' one branch further on. Continue to alternate in this way.

8. Create another woven band of twigs halfway up the tepee, and the final one near the top.

9. Remove the finished tepee from the tub and move to its final location.

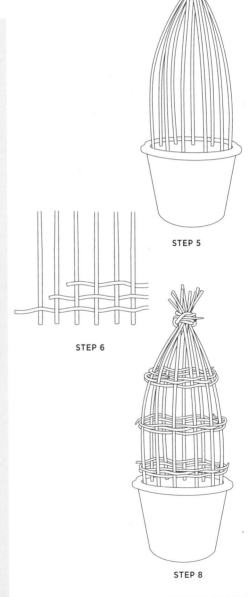

STEP 5

STEP 6

STEP 8

Watering your container plants

Getting watering right is a win-win situation for both your plants and the planet. There are two main challenges. The first is to use (and save) as much rainwater as possible – it's the eco-conscious choice and plants prefer to be watered naturally. The second challenge is to water mindfully.

Water is essential for plants but with containers, too much water is just as bad for a plant as too little – it is important to get it just right. The golden rule is to only water containers when needed. Different plants and containers need different amounts of water. Dig a finger into the compost to check if it's dry.

Use a watering can with a fine rose or a spout to provide a gentle flow of water, and water the base of the plant near the roots and not the leaves. Water slowly, filling the container to the rim until the water drains out of the bottom of the pot. You may need to fill it again to make sure all the compost is moistened.

Water in the morning, as it allows plants to use the water while they are growing during the day. Watering in the evening will leave the soil wet, which could attract slugs and snails as well as provide ideal conditions for fungus.

Rainwater vs tap water

Our changing climate and growing population mean we must learn to cope with water shortages on a regular basis. Our weather is becoming warmer and more volatile, with periods of drought and short bursts of intense rain. This means it's time to turn off the tap when it comes to using water in the garden. This makes sense in other ways, too:

- Plants prefer rainwater, as tap water often has a higher pH.

- Tap water costs money.

- Rainwater is free and there's plenty of it that could be collected.

GO GREENER

Wine barrels from vineyards can be repurposed to use as wooden water butts.

WATER-SAVING TIPS

DO

- Place plants in locations where they will catch the rain.

- Harvest water by installing a water butt, rain chain or even using a large bucket.

- Use drought-resistant planting (such as succulents and herbs) that will need less water.

- Choose soil- or loam-based composts as they retain more water than peat-based ones.

- Mulch your plants so the soil retains more moisture.

- Remove unwanted weeds from containers, as they will compete for water.

- Group containers together to help create shade and humidity.

- Place saucers under containers to capture any water that drains out.

- Reuse water from the house. You could place a small container in the shower as you wait for the water to warm up or in the kitchen sink while rinsing. You can also use 'grey water' from washing dishes or bathing if you use eco-friendly soaps and detergents. Use within 24 hours to avoid bacteria issues.

- Choose finer textured composts for droughty situations such as hanging baskets.

DON'T

- Water without checking to see if the compost is dry. Only water when it is needed.

- Use a hose or sprinkler to water containers.

- Give your container 'just a little' water as it will mean the roots will become shallower.

- Use compost that is too free-draining – water will simply flow straight through the container.

GO GREENER

Avoid watering during the middle of the day on hot summer days – an estimated 25% or more of the water that should be going to your plants will be lost to evaporation and the wind.

Harvesting and using rainwater

Collecting rainwater using sustainable methods is an excellent way of conserving the general water supply, can often save you money on water bills and reduces your environmental impact. When choosing a location for your harvesting system, aim for areas where rainwater runoff collects, such as under roof gutters or out in the open, away from trees. It's also important to keep your gutters clear to optimize flow and insert a mesh screen to filter out leaf debris.

You can collect rainwater in buckets or any type of container, but you will also need a closed storage container if the water is to be used as and when it is needed. The game-changer is to install a water butt – a tank or barrel that can be made of metal or wood,

though most are plastic, so look out for those made of recycled material. They range in size (30–250L; 53–440pt) and can be attached, via pipes, to garage and house roofs, downpipes and greenhouse gutters. An opening towards the bottom dispenses rainwater.

Water butts also come in slender and wall-mounted forms for balconies or small spaces. How much water you need for your containers depends on their size and the plants, but it is quite possible that just one 250L (440pt) water butt, provided that it is refilled periodically by the occasional summer downfall, will provide enough water for 10 medium-sized containers from late spring to early autumn.

Hang a rain chain

A rain chain is a simple but effective method to channel water from a roof or gutter. The chain, which can be made of metal links or a more decorative design, is attached to the eaves or gutters of a house instead of a downpipe. The water flows down the chain and into a barrel or storage container. It can also be positioned over a container rain garden – created and planted with specific perennials and grasses that adapt well to uneven water flows. A rain chain cannot handle heavy rainfall as efficiently as a downspout, although it does sound more mellifluous.

Self-watering methods

Drip trays Water from a filled drip tray or saucer underneath containers will be absorbed into the compost. Capillary matting can also be used. This is only good for a day or two.

Bottling it Fill a bottle or jar with water and, after turning it upside down, bury it partially in the soil. Use a lid with a hole (or two or three) to release as required, or don't use one if you don't mind the water releasing quickly.

Shoelaces Fill a bucket with water and place it on bricks or a box near the container. Put a long shoelace (or two) into the water and put the other end next to the bottom of the plant. The laces will draw up the water for the roots to absorb.

Self-watering pots There are a range of pots with built-in water reservoirs that can be purchased. Most have water indicators to tell you when you will need to top up.

Self-watering irrigation systems Drip-irrigation kits can be put together to deliver water to each container via a timer. Traditionally, the systems are attached to a tap, so look for kits that make it possible to attach to a water butt instead.

Wicking beds These are often used for large water-thirsty vegetable beds. You can purchase a kit or make your own. The basic idea is to create a water reservoir at the bottom of a large container (recycled IBCs are often used) that is linked to an outlet pipe as well as an overflow. It is separated from the compost and plants by root barrier material. A wicking bed will sharply reduce how often you will need to water.

Self-watering (wicking bed)

The basic idea behind a wicking bed is that it allows you to water plants from below rather than above. Think of them as containers with a water reservoir at the bottom. The water is drawn up – or 'wicks up' – through the geotextile and soil via capillary action.

Wicking beds, which ideally range from 1m (3.2ft) to 3.5m (11.5ft) in length, are particularly useful for growing fruit, vegetables and herbs. You will have to invest time and some money in the setup but, depending on size, the soil can remain moist for more than a week at a time – a boon for anyone going on holiday.

A wicking bed acts as a way to future-proof your garden in this climate change era. It also eliminates any chance of leaf scorching, which can happen when you water plants from above, and radically reduces evaporation from the soil.

Wicking beds can both store water and capture rainwater. They are great for absorbing a downpour and studies have shown they will require up to 50 per cent less watering than a conventional bed.

Geotextile fabric covering entire area

Coarse aggregate/ pebbles/gravel

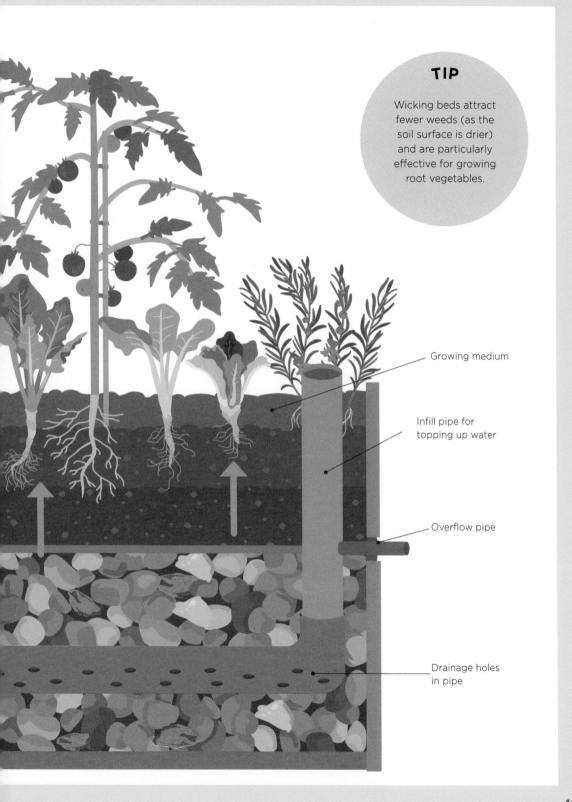

Growing medium

Infill pipe for topping up water

Overflow pipe

Drainage holes in pipe

Feeding your plants

Plants in containers rely on you for the extra nutrients they need. Many nutrients will come from the soil or compost, but most plants will want a regular boost during the growing season. That's where fertilizers come in – use only organic fertilizers, which are better for the planet and provide a long-term supply of nutrients, which is better for the plants.

WHEN FEEDING YOUR PLANTS

DO

- Use organic fertilizers derived from natural ingredients.

- Read labels carefully to make sure there are no inorganic additives.

- Make sure the soil is moist before you feed.

- Think about making your own – it's worth growing a pot of comfrey to make 'tea' from its leaves.

- Feed plants weekly or fortnightly during the spring and summer.

DON'T

- Overfeed your plants, which can result in stunting their growth, or even killing them.

- Feed wildflowers which, in general, prefer to live without any extra boosts.

- Feed plants in the autumn or winter even if they are winter-flowering.

- Feed plants between late autumn and early spring.

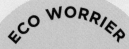

Excess soluble fertilzer can leach nutrients into groundwater, causing pollution. Avoid by using slow-release, organic materials.

Nutrients

The three super or macro-nutrients required in higher quantities by most plants are nitrogen (N), phosphates (P) and potassium (K). When choosing a feed, concentrate on providing the nutrient that each plant needs the most.

Almost all fertilizers contain all three and product labels will give the NPK ratio. Most fertilizers will have high nitrogen, so it's the other two numbers that matter most – for instance, for flowers, K needs to be higher than P. Most proprietary fertilizers will be balanced with the correct levels of each nutrient for the purpose stated on the product label.

Other essential nutrients such as magnesium are required in much smaller quantities, but they can result in deficiencies in specific types of plants, mostly fruit and vegetables.

N: think green Nitrogen is needed for growing leaves, for foliage plants or shrubs and leafy vegetables. Signs of deficiency include yellowing young leaves and lack of growth.

P: think roots Plants with tubers or rhizomes will require phosphates, as will those with storage roots. Signs of deficiency include darker green or brown leaves or those tinged with purple, bronze or red, and those that are stunted or underdeveloped.

K: think flowers and fruit Potassium is needed for controlling water uptake and harnessing sunlight for photosynthesis. A potassium-rich feed encourages flowering and fruiting in various plants, including tomatoes.

A guide to organic feed

Organic fertilizers are slower acting than synthetic formulas. Those that are sprinkled on the soil or compost need to break down and be absorbed by the roots. Liquid feeds are absorbed faster but will need to be used more often.

Seaweed fertilizer A liquid extract, it provides a good balanced feed when diluted.

Wormery Diluted wormery liquid or powder provides a balanced feed.

Hoof and horn A granular by-product of the meat industry, it is used to increase nitrogen.

Bone meal A powdered by-product of the meat industry, it is high in phosphorus and good for root growth.

Fish, blood and bone A powdered by-product of the meat and fish industry, it provides a balanced feed when sprinkled.

Comfrey tea A liquid extract that contains potassium and is good for flowers and fruit.

Nettle tea A liquid extract, contains some nitrogen.

DIY plant food

Comfrey leaves contain a reasonable amount of potassium and if you grow your own, they are free. If you don't have any in your garden, grow some in a pot.

GO GREENER

Comfrey is a plant superhero – its leaves make a good liquid feed, but you can also use them as a mulch or add them (and stalks) to the compost pile.

Here's how to make comfrey 'tea':

1. Remove leaves from plants and fill a bucket with the leaves.

2. Add a drop of water to the bucket and then let them stew in their own juices.

3. If necessary, place a stone on top to make sure the leaves stay compressed.

4. Cover with a lid or a piece of cardboard (it gets very smelly).

5. Check now and again to make sure that the 'tea' is becoming squidgy. If not, add a drop more water.

6. Leave for three to four weeks.

7. Decant the dark liquid from the bucket and keep as plant food.

8. Top up the bucket with fresh leaves and keep moist.

Fertilizer choice

There are many types of fertilizer, but you should only use organic – either purchased or made yourself. They include seaweed, hoof and horn, dried blood, fish blood and bone, and bone meal; homemade 'teas' (from comfrey or nettles); and diluted wormery liquid.

Some concentrated fertilizers (some of which are organic) are good if a more instant supply of nutrients is required, such as for growing hungry vegetable crops such as cucumbers, tomatoes or courgettes.

Stinging nettles are a good nitrogen source and make a good feed for leafy plants. Here's how to make nettle 'tea':

1. Use gloves to strip the leaves off stems.

2. Immerse leaves in a bucket with a general guide of 1kg (2lb) nettles to 10L (21pt) water.

3. Stir daily.

4. Leave for two weeks.

5. Decant.

6. Top up with leaves and water for a continuous supply.

Worm tea makes a good balanced feed. It is made from the worm casings, or poo, also known as vermicompost. Fill your worm bin with a mix of soil and kitchen scraps and add red wiggler worms. Many wormeries have at least two compartments – the lower one will collect liquid. Dilute at a rate of 10 parts water to one part worm liquid, until it is the colour of weak tea.

Working with nature

It is only natural that wildlife of all kinds will want to visit your container garden, and native plants may want to claim a foothold, too. It is up to you how much you accommodate these visitors. For the most part, they will leave little trace, but a few may cause damage and greener strategies may be needed to deter them.

Birds and other wildlife

It would be so much better if birds, squirrels, rabbits and deer shared with us, wouldn't it? Most are unlikely to cause too many issues for your containers – and birds in particular may be welcomed – but here are some green alternatives to use as deterrents if needs be...

Birds Try fakery such as decoy owls, flying falcons and hawks, and toy snakes. You could also use eco-friendly netting such as hemp, voile or wedding net tulle. Bits of bright fabric flying in the wind might do the trick, as might scarecrows – just keep moving them around your garden.

Squirrels Bury chicken wire under the soil surface or spread chilli powder (and other hot spices) in the soil. You can also use chicken wire over the tops of your containers.

Rabbits/deer Locate your containers in out-of-reach areas or behind fences – higher containers will stop rabbits. Plant species that these animals are known to dislike.

GO GREENER

Eco-friendly weed barriers for containers include newspaper or mulch mats made of hemp and other fibres, so you won't need to use those made of woven plastic fibres.

Weeds

A weed for container gardeners can be defined as a plant growing that wasn't planted there by you. If left, they will compete with the other (wanted) plants for resources. One thing to consider, however, is that some of these interlopers are now being seen as 'weed heroes' because of their value to wildlife. You may decide to allow a few to stay, but don't let them take over.

Weed deterrents include a deep bark mulch or using ground-cover plants. You could also put eco-friendly fabric weed barriers in place when planting.

Pull weeds before they set seed. You can pull shallow-rooted annual and ephemeral weeds out by hand or disturb them with a garden fork.

Deep-rooted perennial plants such as dandelions or couch grass need to be completely removed as even a small bit of root will regrow. Use a trowel or grubber.

It may be necessary to remove the compost from the pot in order to get at the roots of tenacious weeds.

Clockwise from top left: dandelion, daisies, thistles, teasel, garlic mustard

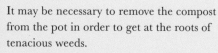

Plant annoyances and diseases

The idea is to work with nature and not against it. Think prevention and you may avoid many problems altogether. You'll need to be alert and vigilant, but remember that many insects are your friends in the fight against your foes.

Smart strategies

Vigilance and regular observation help contain problems:

Prevention The best offence is defence when it comes to avoiding many unwelcome visitors.

Cleanliness Wash tools and pots and disinfect secateurs.

Pruning The '3-D' rule is to cut out any part of the plant that is dead, diseased or damaged. Cut stems at a slant to avoid water sitting on it. For shrubs, prune any crossing branches to encourage air circulation.

Disease-resistant cultivars Seed packets and plant labels will highlight cultivars that are resistant to common diseases and critters.

Know your enemy All critters also have their good points, and many can be tolerated in small doses, but no one likes to see a slug heading for a hosta. Know which you are going to tolerate and those that have to go.

Act quickly At first sight, pick off critters by hand.

Go on night patrol This is when slugs and snails are most active.

Companion planting Some plants protect each other from predators.

Natural pesticides Pesticides based on oils or soaps are effective against small unwanted insects. They leave no residue and are consistent with organic gardening methods.

GO GREENER

'Rehome' slugs and snails at least 20m (66ft) away. Or plant astrantia, a flower that is said to repel slugs.

Natural enemies

The basic rule here is that your enemy's enemy is your friend:

① Hoverflies These harmless insects feast on bugs, including aphids, as do lacewings, ladybirds and their larvae. Consider including their favourite plants such as marigolds and fennel.

② Scale insects Ladybirds and parasitoid wasps feed on these.

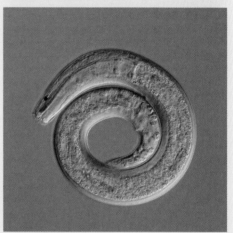

③ Nematodes These are a useful biological control for various enemies including scale insects, vine weevil, slugs and snails. Water them on in late summer to get things under control.

④ Vine weevil They and their grubs are eaten by birds, frogs, toads, shrews, hedgehogs and ground and rove beetles. Other tactics include inspecting plants by torchlight and picking off the adult weevils. Microscopic insect-killing nematodes are another option.

Staying on track

This seasonal guide will help you stay on top of your container garden throughout the year and also look out for wildlife, too. The summer months are busier, but winter is a wonderful time to design a new project.

Autumn

- ☐ Pot up winter container displays.
- ☐ Leave some seedheads and flowerheads for wildlife.
- ☐ Plant spring bulbs.
- ☐ Plant bare-root trees and shrubs.
- ☐ Leave the leaf 'litter' and perhaps even add a few twigs and small branches to create insect habitat in most containers…
- ☐ …except for alpine containers, which need all leaf litter removed.
- ☐ Raise containers onto 'pot feet' or bricks to prevent them standing in water.

Winter

- ☐ Protect tender plants by taking them inside or wrapping them.
- ☐ Wrap frost-vunerable containers in hessian or them take inside.
- ☐ Dream and design a new container garden.
- ☐ Do a winter bird and wildlife survey, counting all you can find in 1 hour.
- ☐ Research and source plants for the coming season.
- ☐ Create natural plant supports.
- ☐ Make solitary bee 'hotels'.
- ☐ Put up bird and bat boxes near your containers.

Spring

- ☐ Clean containers with diluted detergent or vinegar.
- ☐ Check and/or add water butts.
- ☐ Cut back some perennials, including grasses.
- ☐ Sow seeds on windowsills.
- ☐ Pot on overcrowded plants.
- ☐ If not repotting, refresh compost by replacing a third and top-dress.
- ☐ Divide perennials such as hostas.
- ☐ Place plant supports where they will be needed.
- ☐ Mulch the top of your containers.
- ☐ Start weekly feed with an organic fertilizer.
- ☐ Collect comfrey and/or nettle leaves to make fertilizer.
- ☐ Once frost has passed, sow seeds or plant seedlings in situ.
- ☐ Plant summer bulbs.

Summer

- ☐ Organize a holiday watering plan.
- ☐ Continue weekly feed with a natural fertilizer.
- ☐ Harvest 'cut and come again' vegetables and fruit.
- ☐ Patrol for slugs and snails.
- ☐ Tie up climbers on plant supports.
- ☐ Look out for 'weeds' and remove those you don't want.
- ☐ Check containers for moisture every morning, especially on warm or windy days.
- ☐ Deadhead flowering plants.
- ☐ Stake tall annuals such as sunflowers.
- ☐ Do a summer bird and wildlife survey, counting birds and wildlife for an hour.

Creating a container garden

It's inspiration time! The joys of container gardening include the sheer amount of choice on offer when it comes to picking a style or theme. Why not create your own orchard on a patio? Or plant your very own meadow? A container pond can be a game-changer for wildlife. This section provides a guide to the eco-friendly dynamics of designing and creating a container garden and includes user-friendly tips and insights into a wide variety of themes and setups.

Growing in groups

A container garden is more than just one plant in one pot.
From the moment you start to imagine and design your garden,
it makes sense to think in groups. Plants do not live solitary lives
in nature and you will want to reap the many rewards that come
from growing a collection of plants, either in one container or,
indeed, a group of containers.

The rule of numbers

How many containers look 'right' together?
The answer depends on your space and design,
but also pay attention to how the rule of
numbers works. It is generally held that even
numbers create symmetry and a sense of calm.
The downside? They aren't very memorable.

Odd numbers of plants or containers force
your eye to move around the group, and it is
this lingering gaze that means you will be able
to remember it better.

GO GREENER

If you live in a town
or city on a busy road,
a container garden in the
front will soften and
improve the landscape,
promoting wellbeing and
a wildlife oasis.

Little and large choices

One of the first decisions will be the size and number of your containers. Here are a few things to take into consideration:

One large container, many plants...

• Will develop its own microclimate

• Allows for many different sizes of plants

• Is easier to plant in groups or drifts to attract pollinators

• Will be deep enough for a tree or large shrub

• Will make a small space look bigger

• Is easier to water as the larger volume of compost stays moist for longer

Several containers in a variety of sizes...

• Create a microclimate by being placed near each other

• Will attract wildlife that can flow from container to container

• Creates visual appeal

• Can still accommodate a small tree in one larger container

• Are easier to move and arrange in your space

• Are ideal for containing plants such as mint with spreading roots

Larger containers and several of them...

• Are ideal for patio orchards or pocket forests

• Have more scope to mix plants that like sun or shade

• Can act as a pollution screen in a front garden

• Can create an instant 'wow' factor

Ecosystems and habitats in a pot

Containers create habitats with plants interacting with each other, and their environment, as well as the wildlife they attract. There is much more to any garden than meets the eye and it is helpful, when creating your containers, to think of these aspects, as well as the more obvious aesthetics of colour and style.

What plants prefer

One way to see how plants interact is to see a container garden from their point of view. What sort of environment does your set of plants want? You can do the same for wildlife.

◗ Humidity lovers want to be close to other plants, while alpines want to be left with plenty of room.

Companion plants will help each other by repelling or attracting insects, and is particularly useful for edible crops.

◗ Balcony plants will benefit from a nearby plant windbreak, and you can use shade from an adjacent tree or shrub.

Bees like uncomplicated single flowers, while butterflies prefer groups of plants as they are easier to find.

◗ Birds (like this great tit) want seedheads to be left over winter; dragonflies need water to reproduce.

'Wildlife hotel' plants such as ivy provide multiple benefits.

Group dynamics

Humidity All plants release moisture, which evaporates into the air. When placed near each other, plants will produce a cumulative moisture that will increase the humidity around them.

Levels Plants placed at different levels, either by arranging in a container or by placing varying heights of container next to each other, means that excess water will drip onto lower plants.

◗ Pollinator friends Plant bee magnets such as borage or marigolds near edibles like strawberries and courgettes (whose flower can be partially hidden) to help pollination.

Companions Some plants can work well together to deter pests. Marigolds secrete limonene – a scented substance that can repel whitefly – useful around edibles such as beans. They also attract beneficial insects, including ladybirds, which love to eat aphids.

Planting considerations

Think permanent Planting perennials, shrubs or trees means that they will absorb carbon for a longer period than short-lived annual bedding.

◖ Colour coding What mood are you trying to evoke? Do you fancy 'hot' red and orange colours to jazz up a space or something 'cool' such as darker purples and blues to enhance a feeling of calm? You may prefer the 'no colour' look, which is mostly greens and whites.

Wildlife Factor in wildlife considerations from the start and include flowers that are most attractive to certain bees or butterflies.

Foliage Contrasting leaf textures and colours (including variegated) add interest.

Choosing a theme

Now comes the fun part: picking a theme and deciding what your garden is going to look like. Natural or formal? Flower meadow or perhaps a potager that mixes both ornamentals and edibles? There are so many options, but it's important to make sure that your choices chime with the space and containers themselves, as well as your own likes and aims.

Selecting a style

Natural Flowing grasses and perennials as seen in the prairie look and inspired by Piet Oudolf. This also includes cottage gardens and 'nectar' plantings.

Formal Symmetrical and ordered, often featuring clipped balls or shapes, in evergreens such as holly or lavender. Could include a small tree and underplanting.

Traditional Colourful annual bedding, changed seasonally, a style that can be adapted to include mostly perennials with some seasonal changes.

⊕ **Tropical** Lush look with large-leaved, brightly coloured plants and trees as in (below) a large banana surroundedby a riot of colour, including giant marigolds, pink *Nicotiana* (tobacco) flowers and silvery dusty miller.

Garden arrangement

The key to success lies in the mantra 'right plant, right place, right container'. Your theme needs to chime with the characteristics of the space you have and the given location:

• Location aspect

• Sun and shade

• Exposure

• Size of containers

• Number of containers

TIP

Experiment with new styles but don't be swayed by fashionable ideas that go against your personal dislikes. If you like formality, then a 'messy-looking' grassy meadow planting may make you feel uncomfortable.

Dry Alpines and succulents in a 'dry' container.

☽ **Mediterranean** Drought-tolerant plants that include many herbs such as rosemary and thyme, as well as lavenders.

Forest Trees and shrubs in large containers to create a high-impact 'forest bathing' space.

☽ **Shady** Ferns and hostas in a wet and cool corner, often featuring mostly green plants with splashes of colour.

Double-check space

Now is the time to make sure that the selected containers will actually fit into the location you have chosen. Weight limits are particularly important for balconies – this is usually calculated at 70kg per square metre (154lb per square foot). Consider consulting a structural engineer for ambitious schemes.

Different designs

The classic design formula for a small patio container has been 'thriller, filler, spiller', which involves one tall focal point surrounded by mid-sized plants with trailers near the edges. Containers are much more versatile these days and can be assessed in much wider terms when it comes to style and design.

The delicate flowers of the purple bell vine trail over the side of this pot

TIP

There is no need for a container garden to match the style of your wider garden or landscape, and indeed, a contrast can add to its attraction.

GETTING IT RIGHT

DO

- Be willing to try something new or different.

- Make sure your theme works for the space and location.

- Choose a colour scheme that reflects your 'mood' goal.

- Factor in wildlife considerations from the start.

- Think about vertical space.

DON'T

- Choose a style just because it's fashionable.

- Use conflicting styles in one container.

- Fill your container with lots of individual plants.

- Use only annuals that need constant replacement.

Theme considerations

Unity Plants should complement or contrast well with each other and, when placed together, look as if they belong together.

Layers and levels Using small, medium and tall plants creates extra interest and gives an impression of complexity.

Balance Make sure the container isn't lopsided with, for instance, lots of colour on one side, and none on the other.

Vertical space Use height with a tree or tepee climber to create drama and a focal point.

Repetition Use more than one plant of each type and, if room, use them in more than one place in a container.

⊕ Edges Soften the edges by tilting plants or by using trailing plants such as *Ilex crenata* and *Geranium* 'Rozanne' as shown below.

Creating a plan for your container garden

It is tempting to 'wing it' when it comes to creating a planting plan and designing your garden, but the result can be less than satisfactory. The process of drawing up a plan and making a list of desirable plants makes it easier to spot any gaps or issues early on.

Think visually

Often designers will say they can 'see' what something will look like before it exists. You may believe that you can't 'think visually', but this is a skill that can be nurtured and developed with certain practices.

Try to make it a practice to draw on a regular basis – it helps to keep a weekly 'drawing' diary. Imagine plant combinations and draw them using the right dimensions. Also start to think of percentages or numbers as displayed in a chart or graph.

Make a list of your 'must-have' plants

You already have your theme and probably a good idea of what kind of plants you would like to include. It may seem fussy to write them down, but this will save you time and effort in the long run. For every plant, list:

- Name

- Height

- Colour

- Wildlife possibilities

- Other seasonal attributes

How to create your planting plan

Measure your containers and write down length, width and depth. Scale the measurements so that you can record them accurately on paper. For instance, one square of graph paper could represent 10cm (4in). Scale rulers can also be used if you are using blank paper.

⚊ **A bird's eye view or layout plan** is your container garden as seen from directly above. Draw it out using the width and length measurements, then use tracing paper placed over it to experiment with various designs. This allows for more experimentation than just using a pencil on the original paper. Assign each of your 'must-have' plants a symbol or colour so you can see drifts, and so on. Try out several different plans, varying placements.

⚊ **The side view or elevation plan** is as seen from ground level directly in front. Draw it out using height and length measurements, then cover it with tracing paper. Draw the height of the plants in your plan, and don't forget to draw in any plant supports.

You could go further and create a mood board using photos, cutouts from magazines and other items. Sketch out, in 3-D, what the finished container will look like. Use watercolours or water-soluble pencils to see colour themes.

SKETCHING A PLAN

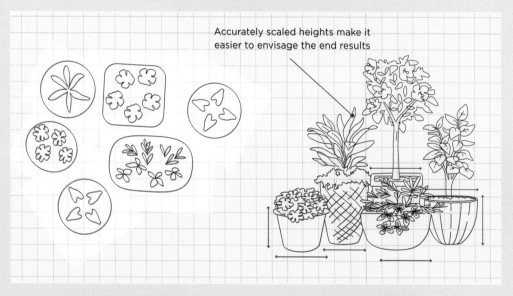

Accurately scaled heights make it easier to envisage the end results

A BIRD'S EYE VIEW   **ELEVATION PLAN**

Get creative

Your planting plans can be as sketchy or as detailed as you like. It is important to have the correct basic measurements of your containers, as that will be the key to making the design work, but there is no need to get bogged down in trying to make it look perfect.

Innovative ideas

1. **See the patterns** Use different symbols and colours to depict the location of plants in your containers. This makes it easy, in a bird's eye view layout, for you to see planting patterns, and to recognize where repetition might help bring balance (and wildlife) to your container.

2. **Make a wildlife map** Any planting plan can be transformed into a 'wildlife map' by copying it and then depicting what kind of pollinators or wildlife certain plants are going to attract.

3. **Succession planting** Sketching out what will be in flower in spring, summer and autumn/winter makes it easy to see the gaps in terms of all-season interest.

4. **Going up** An elevation plan determines if you are missing layers. Even in a prairie or meadow container, you will want plants of different heights to give a layered effect.

5. **Step back and assess** It is often at the very end of the process that you look at your plan and realize that it is missing something. Are your plants too small or predictable? Is there is enough colour and contrast? Are you missing the wow factor?

Tepees add height and structure

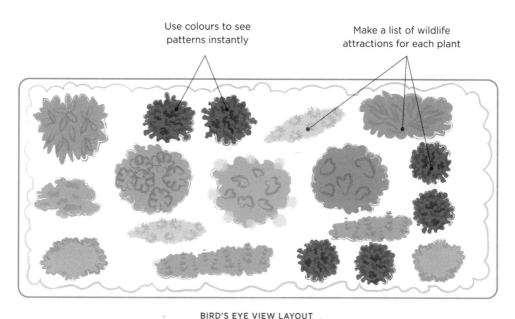

Use colours to see patterns instantly

Make a list of wildlife attractions for each plant

BIRD'S EYE VIEW LAYOUT

Climbers provide extra interest for pollinators

Bringing it all together

- Make your final plant list.

- Tick off how to acquire them.

- Buy or swap seeds and plants.

- Don't be sidetracked by random gorgeous blooms at the garden centre.

- Place plants still in pots in containers.

- Don't be afraid to experiment with placement.

- Plant!

Creating eco habitats

The garden you create is not just for you but also for wildlife and, in the bigger picture, the planet. We are used to thinking about plants in terms of colour and flower power, but it is also part of greener gardening to see what they mean for wildlife and wellbeing.

The container garden ecosystem

- Containers and/or plants near each other create their own microclimates.

- Companion planting supports plant health.

- Edible plants mean fewer food miles.

- Planting for pollinators aids all wildlife.

- Trees and shrubs remove more carbon dioxide from the air.

- Adding a container pond enhances wildlife diversity.

The bigger picture

A container garden doesn't exist in a vacuum, and its surroundings – or borrowed landscape as garden designers think of it – are linked to it as well. Is there something, such as a pond or a herb garden, that your current garden is lacking that a container garden can provide? What it sits next to, be it a wall or a border or a lawn, will have an influence on it and vice versa. A container garden can help with issues such as front garden pollution or, if placed near a wall with a climber such as ivy, can help regulate temperatures in buildings. It can be a nectar boost, an edible patch, a colourful mood enhancer.

Attracting wildlife

When planning your planting, put wildlife into the equation. It's a virtuous cycle. Pollinators on the lookout for nectar plants will then pollinate other plants. Encourage insects and you provide food for birds and allow the likes of ladybirds to get busy eating aphids.

Here are some easy ways to attract the wild ones into all types of container gardens:

- Extend the flowering season to help pollinators.

- Plant single flowers to lure bees, which prefer them to double flowers.

- Attract dragonflies and damselflies with winter containers.

- Provide birds with plants that produce winter berries and seeds, as they love them.

- Plant a variety of nectar plants for butterflies. Some plants are used specifically by individual butterfly species.

- Consider keeping some so-called weeds, such as nettles and dandelions, which are wildlife magnets.

EXTRA PLUSES FOR WILDLIFE

DO

- Create a small water basin with pebbles for pollinators.

- Create a ladder for frogs to get in and out of a pond inside a container (see page 106).

- Place houses for birds, bats and butterflies nearby.

- Create small piles of twigs/branches for insects.

- Make a 'hotel' for solitary bees.

DON'T

- Be too tidy in autumn, allowing leaves for overwintering insects.

- Use pesticides as they can harm beneficial insects as well.

- Plant only one type of plant in a container.

- Use only seasonal annuals.

ECO WORRIER

Conduct a wildlife survey of your garden in summer and winter for a record of visitors like this song thrush enjoying rowan berries.

Eco-friendly game-changers

Your container garden may look too beautiful to be so hardworking, but it will be a natural multitasker that also provides food for wildlife and benefits to the wider environment, too. Here are some ideas that provide that extra boost for all...

Edibles There is a vast array of edibles that can be grown in containers, providing delicious food for you and cutting food travel miles. Dwarf fruit trees provide a perfect combination of saving carbon, while also providing delicious treats. All edible perennials do that trick, too. Annual edimentals, such as climbing beans, look and taste great (and attract wildlife, too).

A container pond Crucial for adding a new dimension to any garden. On its own, it will provide a home for different plants and wildlife, as well as foster a sense of calm. When placed in a group of containers, it adds something special to the mix. For instance, in a wild edible container garden, a pond will provide the likes of watercress and water mint. In addition, it will attract dragonflies, water insects and even, perhaps, a frog or two.

A tree All plants pull carbon out of the air and store it in their leaves, roots and stems. The bigger the better when it comes to carbon storage, which is why trees are such a boon to fighting climate change. A small tree punches way above its weight in any container, providing beauty and shade, as well as attracting all sorts of insects. If there is no room for a tree, shrubs and indeed groups of perennials will provide extra carbon storage.

TIP

Strawberries can sit nicely amid other non-edible plants, adding colour as well as tasty treats in summer.

Water adds beauty and movement and is a major attraction for wildlife.

Hawthorn trees offer glorious colour and provide wonderful food for pollinators in spring, and birds in autumn.

Superlative wildlife plants

- Sunflowers (flowers and seeds)

- Ivy (flowers, fruit and habitat)

- Hawthorn (flowers and fruit)

- Native wildflowers (flowers)

- Nettles (flowers and habitat)

- Teasel (flowers and seeds)

- Sedum (flowers and seeds)

Setting up a container pocket forest

Every garden should have at least one tree, but creating a container pocket forest goes further. The idea is inspired by the late Japanese botanist Akira Miyawaki, who created pocket forests with closely planted native trees, so the plant layers naturally work together to create their own ecosystem, attracting more birds and insects, reducing air and noise pollution and absorbing carbon. You'll need a large container for this.

Planning your pocket forest

Space Pocket forests can be created in almost any space, as long as it is a few metres square. Large containers placed in a small space make the area look bigger and the height of the trees will add another dimension, creating a sense of privacy and feeling of immersion.

Plant layers Think in terms of traditional forest layers of canopy, underlayer, field and floor. You can adapt this to your container by grouping a tree with a multi-stem shrub, such as elderflower, with a field layer of small ferns and bulbs, and a ground layer of mosses and, perhaps, ivy.

Containers Aim for the containers to be at least 1m² (11ft²) and, crucially, 1m (3ft) deep. Options include metal salvage tanks or larger stone and terracotta pots, but one of the most practical are industrial IBCs. These are large and adaptable.

Two containers, placed near to each other, will be able to accommodate at least two trees plus other shrubs and plants.

Drainage, soil and care Drainage is key and you will need to drill holes in the bottom of any recycled containers. You will also need a substantial bottom layer of gravel.

Use loam-based, peat-free compost and, given the dimensions, buy in bulk. Refresh the top layer of compost annually in spring, adding at least 5cm (2in) of new material.

TIP

Join in the Japanese practice of forest bathing – it's all about being calm and quiet among the trees, observing the greenery while breathing deeply.

Opposite: These Intermediate Bulk Containers (IBCs) have been planted with Asplenium scolopendrium, Dryopteris, Polystichum *and* Astrantia.

Trees and plants to try

Trees Hazel, rowan, crab apple and hawthorn can all be found in smaller sizes. All have flowers and fruit that will attract wildlife and will look good for more than just one season.

Shrubs Elderflower, dog rose and cornus are among those that grow to several metres but, as they are multi-stemmed, they will be rounder and complement the shape of a tree.

Field layer Cardoon is a striking architectural silver-leaved member of the daisy family; the tassels on sweetcorn provide added interest; trailing nasturtiums offer long-lasting colour – and their flowers and seeds are edible.

Herbs Fennel and dill for their feathery foliage; thyme (which comes in many leaf colours) and chives are good ground cover; parsley can be interplanted.

All-year interest Winter hardy kale and cabbages, and evergreen herbs such as rosemary and sage will look good all winter long.

GO GREENER

Buy bare-root plants, available in the autumn and winter, if possible. Not only do they cost less, but they also have far less plastic packaging.

Hazel and sorbus pocket forest

This pocket forest, planting in repurposed industrial IBC containers, is made up of layers that will benefit wildlife and the planet as well as providing a calm green space. Here, two 1m-deep (3ft) containers have been planted with hazel, hawthorn and birch, with elderflower and cornus shrubs, ferns, bluebells and other flowers. Anyone for a spot of forest bathing on your own back patio?

Choosing what to grow

1. Don't feel obliged to restrict yourself to choosing the common version of a native tree. Sometimes a variety can provide an extra touch of colour or a smaller size. For instance, *Betula utilis* subsp. *jacquemontii* 'Doorenbos', has stunning white bark.

2. Always look for multi-season interest when picking a tree. Hazel, for instance, has pendulous catkins in the early spring, bright green leaves that turn yellow in the autumn and small nuts. It's also beloved by moths and caterpillars, which birds love.

3. Some trees, such as hawthorn, can also be maintained at shrub size, and are a magnet for wildlife. The hawthorn's multi-season interest includes white spring flowers (there are pink and red varieties, too) that turn to haws in the autumn, which you can use to make jams and jellies.

4. Think permanent – a pocket forest should be seen as a long-lasting display that will grow and mature over the years, creating canopy and shade. Permanent plantings absorb carbon over the longest period and generally require less compost, water and feeding.

5. The field layer, with its grasses and ferns, will create a feeling of lushness. Some native wildflowers, such as aquilegia, grow well in shade and can be used in the underplanting.

6. The ground layer, with its moss and lichen, will develop over time. Dead leaves and small branches can be left to decompose, creating a habitat for more insects and adding to soil health.

TIP

Even if they are small now, some trees like oak and beech will grow much too big in the end.

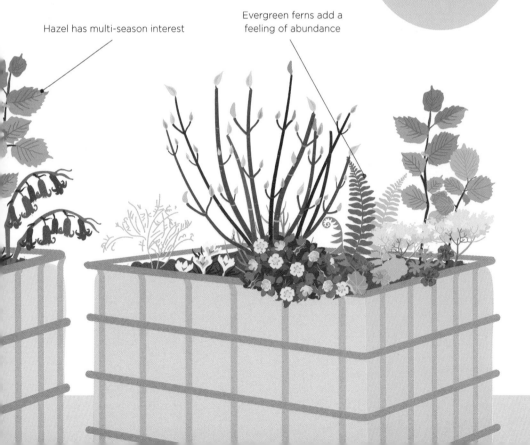

Hazel has multi-season interest

Evergreen ferns add a feeling of abundance

Putting together a patio orchard

You do not need to own a field to have an orchard. If you choose the right-sized trees, and look after them, you can grow a thriving mini orchard on your patio. Orchards are wonderful creations, useful, beautiful and great for wildlife, too.

TIP

Sheltered gardens are less prone to spring frosts and retain the sun's heat well – perfect for growing plants that love warmth.

Planning your patio orchard

Space Choose a sunny, sheltered area. The space required depends to some extent on the shape of your trees. Options include the traditional shape as well as 'columnar' (super-skinny), fan, cordon or espalier.

Containers You will need stable pots that are at least 45–50cm (18–20in) in diameter. Terracotta, stone or metal can work, or reuse and upcycle old plastic pots. It is important to get the right initial size as overpotting (a pot that is too big) may affect the health of the tree, as the roots will sit for too long in wet compost.

Soil, drainage and care Use good-quality loam-based compost such as John Innes No 3 or a multipurpose one. Mix in some grit until it makes up a third. The grit in the soil will aid drainage. Place crocks at the bottom. Use a high-potassium liquid feed once a week or every other week in the growing season.

Trees and rootstock The most important thing is to choose fruit that you love to eat. Then you need to find cultivars suited to containers. These will be trees that have been grafted onto a rootstock that will limit size and vigour (see box). When buying, the tree should be labelled as a compact variety and list the rootstock.

Trees and shrubs

While some fruit trees are self-fertile, that is, they don't require another tree for pollination, do need to be grown with a pollination group pair. For instance, when choosing apples, you could pair the culinary 'Arthur Turner' with the dessert 'Discovery', both of which are in group 3. (The numbers reflect the time of year it flowers.) You will need to stick with apples (as plums or pears in the same group will not do the trick). If you only want one apple tree, then choose a self-fertile one.

Apples Cooking include 'Arthur Turner' and 'Bountiful' (both 3) and dessert ones include 'Discovery', 'Falstaff', 'Sunset' (all 3) and 'Pixie' (4).

Stone fruit Apricots ('Delicot', 'Moorpark'), cherries ('Lapins', 'Stella'), peaches ('Garden Lady', 'Peregrine'), plums ('Dessert Opal', 'Victoria') and nectarines ('Nectarella') are all self-fertile.

Pears and quince Pears 'Conference' (3) and 'Doyenne du Comice' (4); 'Sibley's Patio Quince'.

Shrubs and vines Blueberries 'Northsky', 'Northcountry'), grapes ('Seyval Blanc', 'Siegerrebe') and gooseberries ('Greenfinch').

Patio orchard rootstocks

Apricot St Julian A or Torinel

Apple M9, M26 (M27 is too small)

Cherry Colt or Gisela 5

Pear Quince C

Plum and peach Pixy or St Julian A

Eco-friendly patio orchard

A patio orchard is one of the most eco-friendly things you can create. It is attractive, stores carbon, provides food and thus reduces food miles and expense. In addition, it is adored by bees and other pollinators as well as birds.

Choosing what to grow

1. Pollination is key for an orchard of any size and including a pot of pollinator-friendly perennial flowers will help things along. Place these among your trees and sit back and listen for the buzz.

2. Some unusual fruit isn't as available commercially as others. If you like gooseberries, or the lesser-known medlar or quince, then grow them yourself. It's also fun to try something different. Pomegranate, anyone?

3. Think long season and plan so the fruiting season lasts from the first blueberry or cherry to the last apple or even quince; it will mean months of fresh fruit at your fingertips.

4. Be patient, as it can take some fruit trees a few years to start to produce and many will produce only a few fruits in the first years. Be sure to plant early, before flowering. Extra pollinators can help, too, as does regular feeding.

Bee-friendly perennial pots provide a pollination boost

5. Try different tree shapes. Varieties such as fan and espaliers can be grown against a wall or fence, but can also be freestanding using a bamboo or metal frame, which looks particularly dramatic.

6. Stepover apples and pears are grown on miniature rootstocks that have been trained into a very low shape. They are usually between 45–60cm (18–24in) high and can work in containers.

Fruit trees benefit from regular feeding during spring and summer

Creating a flowery meadow in a pot

Summer meadows bursting with colour and movement are a joy to see. An impressionistic mini meadow will give any space that romantic tousled look and, with the right choice of plants, can work in sun or shade. Perennial, annual, native or non-native, softly coloured or bigger and bolder – it's up to you; bees, insects and birds will love it just as much as you will.

Planning your flower meadow

Location Make sure you know the chosen location in terms of how much sun and shade it gets. Select plants accordingly and think long term.

Containers A meadow can be created on any scale and, if you have space constraints or are on a balcony, they can still look good in something as small as a window box. A larger container will allow you to use a wider variety of plants and feature spring and summer seasonal colour.

GO GREENER

Cut your mini meadow in late winter to allow the flowers to complete their cycle of growing, flowering and setting seed. The birds will like the winter seed, too.

For smaller spaces, you could plant up smaller containers with one or two plants each and group them together.

Soil and drainage Wildflowers and meadow flowers prefer low-nutrient soil. Topsoil and compost will be too rich and most garden and farm soils are also enhanced. You can reduce the overall nutrient level by mixing in some sand and grit (which helps with drainage as well).

With garden soil, dig down to find the subsoil and use that or top some poor soil with sand or another inert substrate. You can also buy low-nutrient topsoil aimed specifically at wildflowers. Make sure there are adequate drainage holes (meadow flowers won't like being waterlogged) and add a layer of gravel along the bottom.

Plant choices

You have a choice of annuals, biennials and perennials. Meadow wildflowers are relatively tall (at least 30cm; 12in) and thin with flowers in softer pastel colours. For a brighter or bolder look, add a non-UK native such as a sunflower or cosmos – but make sure any non-natives are not invasive.

Choose your plants according to sun and shade. There are many ready-made meadow mixes for sale, including those for shade and coastal areas.

Plants to try

Native cornfield annual wildflowers Cornflowers, corn cockle, corn chamomile, ox-eye daisy and common poppy.

Native wildflower meadow perennials Red campion, wild burnet, field scabious, wild carrot, marjoram, knapweed and honesty.

A favourite non-native Sunflowers will give your meadow height, vibrant colour and seed for birds.

⊕ Vibrant colour Cosmos (annual) will flower for months, and California poppy has zingy orange flowers.

Spring it up Most meadow plants start flowering in late spring, so plant up a lower layer with the likes of cowslips and native bluebells to provide early interest.

Mini meadow

This mini meadow, planted in a recycled metal bath, is placed in a spot that is mostly sunny but with some afternoon partial shade. It is designed with the 'wow factor' in terms of colour and longevity, but also with wildlife in mind. This combination will be particularly attractive to certain butterflies that are struggling now.

Meadow plant mix

1. This meadow mix features mostly native wildflowers of slightly different heights with colours that contrast well: wild carrot (white), marjoram (dark pink), common poppies (red), cornflowers (blue), field scabious (light blue), wild burnet (blood red) and cosmos (white and pink). Fennel has been added for height and seedheads, as its flowers are small and yellow.

2. Think permanent – this mix is mostly perennials or self-seeding annuals, but every year it can be augmented with other annuals, which allows for experimentation. Be aware that, in the second or third year, different species may predominate. A few 'weeds' may also appear; consider leaving them if they are not too dominant or invasive.

3. Some of the UK's less-common butterflies will thank you for planting their favourite meadow natives such as wild marjoram (large blue butterfly) or field scabious (marsh fritillary).

4. When choosing plants, look out for those with autumn and winter interest. Seedheads can look majestic in the autumn and will look particularly striking after a light dusting of snow.

5. Grow your own wildflowers from seed sown outdoors in spring or autumn. They are the ultimate 'no-fuss' plants, which require no extra attention. Annuals look great in the first year, but perennials can take another year to establish and so you may decide to purchase (or swap) for some plug plants.

6. Meadows are at their most beautiful when they are caught in the breeze, their colours intermingling, their stems bending. Think about this when designing your meadow, with different heights that will look good blowing in the wind.

ECO WORRIER

Your mini meadow doesn't need fertilizing or feeding – it will only make your wildflowers unhappy and create an invitation for grasses and weeds.

Establishing a nectar café

The decline of bees and butterflies, as well as other pollinators, is directly linked to a lack of habitat and, therefore, food. The purpose of a nectar café or 'bar' is to provide a garden that specifically caters to pollinators by providing a succession of the kind of flowers that they prefer.

Planning your nectar café

Location Bees and butterflies like a warm and sunny spot that is sheltered from the wind (but not the rain). If you feel nervous around bees, then choose a location that is not right next to where you will be sitting or eating al fresco.

Containers You can create a nectar café or 'bar' in something as small as a window box or as large as a water tank or raised bed. If you have the space, then go large as this will give you room for a variety of nectar-rich plants that will flower from early spring to autumn.

Soil and drainage Use compost that is not overly rich and is peat free and pH neutral. Avoid waterlogged plants with good drainage and adding grit to soil. Feed with a natural fertilizer such as comfrey or nettle once a week during the growing season.

The customers

Bumblebees The UK has 24 species of bumblebee. Most common include tree, red-tailed, white-tailed and carder.

Solitary bees These include masons, who like to live in cavities in wood and brick walls, and mining who live in the ground.

Honeybees The UK has one species of honeybee, which has been domesticated for centuries and lives in hives with up to 30–40,000 others.

Hoverflies Highly prolific pollinators, some are migratory and can travel hundreds of kilometres a day.

Butterflies There are 59 species of butterfly in the UK, with 80 per cent having declined in abundance or range since 1976.

Moths The UK's larger moths declined by 33 per cent between 1968 and 2017. The extent of the losses has worsened in the past decade.

ECO WORRIER

Check that the plants you select all prefer the same soil type. Mismatched plants may not grow properly or even die completely.

What's on the flower menu?

To have plants in bloom from early spring through the end of autumn, you'll need a successional planting plan. Flowers should not have overly elaborate petals, or double layers, which make it harder for pollinators and contain less nectar. If you have the room, a variety of flowers will appeal to a wider selection of butterflies and moths.

Plants to try

◐ **Early season** Aubretia, English bluebell, grape hyacinth, lungwort, primrose and sweet rocket.

◑ **Mid-season** Thyme, fennel, borage, lavender, sea holly, salvias, daisies, common mallow and cosmos.

◐ **Late season** Dahlias, coneflower, honeysuckle, French marigolds, ivy, Michaelmas daisies and common sunflowers.

◐ **For butterflies** Buddleja, *Verbena bonariensis*, marjoram and wallflowers ('Bowles Mauve' is a favourite).

◐ **For moths** Night-scented plants include types of tobacco plant and evening primrose.

Welcome to the 'nectar bar'

This 'nectar bar', or café, caters for a broad range of bees and butterflies, as well as some moths. It's a mutually beneficial arrangement – as the bees and butterflies fly from flower to flower, they are also pollinating them.

How to attract wildlife

1. A nectar café works best when it has been designed and planned to get maximum flower power for the maximum number of days. Otherwise, it's common to end up with mostly summer flowers and hardly anything in early spring or late autumn.

2. When designing your plan, think about colour and height. This mix features mostly soft blues and purples plus yellow and white. Plants for such a mix include: (spring) English bluebell, primrose, grape hyacinth and sweet rocket; (summer) buddleja, borage, marigolds, cosmos, daisies, marjoram, fennel and honeysuckle; (autumn) asters, rudbeckias and sunflowers.

3. Instead of dotting plants around without planning or using just one kind of plant, plant in clumps (ideally at least three) or drifts, as this makes it easier for pollinators to spot the food source. Do this in small containers, such as window boxes, by twinning plants.

4. If in doubt about what plants to include, herbs such as chives, thyme, hyssop, marjoram, fennel and caraway are magnets for bees and butterflies.

Natural plant supports always blend in well

GO GREENER

Stinging nettles are a food source for the caterpillars of some of the UK's most colourful butterflies. They don't have showy flowers but could be planted in a separate container nearby.

5. Night-scented plants will lure moths. Try evening primrose, jasmine, honeysuckle, night-scented stock and tobacco plant *Nicotiana alata.*

6. Think about other ways to cater for your nectar customers. Place a 'puddle' for butterflies and bees – that is, a saucer filled with gravel and small stones and add some rainwater – in your container. Or make a 'hotel' with a collection of tubes that will attract solitary bees and place it nearby.

Butterflies will appreciate a 'puddle' of water

Wild edibles in pots

This is a container garden that is full of tasty surprises – wild edible plants can provide ingredients for homemade jellies and jams, cordials and teas, soups and salads. It's a perfect container planting for those who enjoy experimenting in the kitchen. It can also be a place to forage, as well as providing an intriguing patch of wildness that will also be enjoyed by bees and butterflies.

Elements to consider

Location Choose a location that is mostly sunny but has some shade during the day. Wild edibles are resilient, but they will grow best in a sheltered place. On a practical level, think about placing this near the kitchen or barbecue area.

Containers A larger container means you will be able to grow a small tree or shrub, such as a crab apple or elderflower. An ideal setup would involve three containers: one large (with a shrub or tree) and two others that would receive more sun for salad flower power and herbs.

The flowers of Rosa canina, *or dog rose, can be eaten in salads, made into a syrup or preserved in vinegar.*

Soil and care

Soil should be low-nutrient and include grit or sand. Use a diluted comfrey tea feed to encourage fruiting and flowering. You will deadhead naturally as you forage.

Plants There is a wide choice of plants you could choose from to tailor to your culinary likes. Themes could include a 'cocktail' garden (using flowers from borage, mint, roses, and so on) or 'salad and soup' variety (leaves and flowers from fennel, sorrel, dog rose, nasturtium, and the like).

Whatever your theme, this is also a natural bee and butterfly garden and, as you can also have an edible aquatics tub, you might see a dragonfly or two.

Watercress, which requires moist conditions, can be used in soups and salads.

Plants to try

Trees or large shrubs Crab apple (fruit for jelly), birch (sap for beer) and elderflower (flowers and berries for cordial and jelly).

Fruit Wild strawberry, blackberry, sea buckthorn, wild raspberry, roses (hips) and hawthorn (haws) – for desserts, jellies, jam and syrups.

Edible petals Nasturtiums, wild roses (dog, field, burnet, sweetbriar), borage, clover and mint.

Wild herbs Marjoram, fennel, thyme and rosemary.

Tea Fennel, mint, dandelion and red clover.

Liquorice flavours Wild chervil, sweet cicely and anise hyssop (also called liquorice mint).

Aquatic edibles Watercress, water mint, flowering rush and waterlilies.

Setting up a potager pot plot

The French word *potager* is defined as a 'small kitchen garden' with the idea that it includes plants to be used for the soup (*potage*) pot. This hardly does justice to a garden that bursts with abundance and provides a delightful mix of the productive and decorative. It's fun to create a cornucopia of colour and texture, and it's a haven of biodiversity and is tasty, too.

Elements to consider

Space Look for a spot that offers up to eight hours a day of sun, but where there is also some shade for part of the morning or afternoon. It also needs to be sheltered from the wind but open to receive rain, as this will be a thirsty mix of plants.

Containers A large container (up to 1m (3ft) long and 0.5m (1.6ft) wide) will provide room to grow an innovative mix. Or you could group three medium-sized containers near each other to create one beneficial ecosystem.

TIP

Strong-smelling herbs such as rosemary, thyme and sage might deter cabbage white butterflies, the scourge of brassicas.

Drainage, soil and care Use good peat-free compost, homemade or bought – your plants will want all the nutrients they can get. Refresh the compost annually and mulch regularly to keep weeds down.

Good drainage is essential, so use gravel and crocks at the bottom. Use a natural feed such as seaweed or comfrey regularly during the growing season.

Design and plant choice Make a list of good-looking fruit and vegetables and don't be afraid of the height you would get with globe artichokes, fennel or even a small fruit tree. Experiment with colourful companion plants such as marigolds, and edibles such as nasturtiums.

Plug any gaps with colourful lettuce or quick-growing radishes. Try to include some vegetables that look good throughout the winter, such as black kale.

Plants to try

⊘ **Fruit** Dwarf apples (shown), pears or plums can provide focal points; strawberries are good for ground cover; apples are a talking point; blackberries can trail over an edge.

Vegetables Varieties with extra colour include chard 'Bright Lights', beetroot 'Rainbow Beet', crimson beans, purple peas, multicoloured radishes; and cabbages, squash and lettuce come in many colours.

Herbs Fennel, dill, thyme, chives and parsley.

Flowers Sweet peas, roses of all kinds, lavender, nepeta, thistles, echinacea, honesty, poppies, primroses, sunflowers, cornflowers and hollyhocks.

Perfect for potager Cardoons or globe artichokes, sweetcorn and trailing nasturtiums.

All-year interest Winter-hardy kale and cabbages, and evergreen herbs such as rosemary and sage.

Planting a potager plot

This potager 'plot' uses homemade plant supports to enable even more fruit and vegetables to be grown in a large, wooden, raised bed planter. There is room for sweet peas, runner beans, bronze fennel and silvery globe artichokes. Rainbow chard and radishes are dazzling and look good against a backdrop of black kale. Other plants include lettuce, parsley, chives, rosemary, dog rose and vibrant poppies.

Choosing potager plants

1. Think 'up' when it comes to designing your potager. Use natural plant supports to make tunnels and tepees or, if you have room, an arch. A vertical apple cordon or small pear tree would also add structure, height and interest. Aim for a container with a depth of at least 40cm (16in).

2. Colours can be exuberant. There are many 'rainbow' vegetables out there, including chard, beets and radishes. Many heirloom varieties are multicoloured. Flowers that go 'pop' include echinacea, sunflowers and cornflower.

3. Potagers are perfect for interplanting, which is where you pair up fast-growing plants such as lettuce and beets with the slower-growing sweetcorn and broccoli.

4. Companion planting is a natural way to protect your plants. Aphids are said to dislike marigolds and nepeta (catmint). Onions, leeks and chives are believed to deter carrot fly. Dill, coriander and nasturtiums can be planted with kale, which may discourage caterpillars.

Mixing vegetables and flowering climbers add interest

5. A potager garden attracts wildlife, particularly bees and butterflies, as the succession of blooms and the variety, lasting over months, is a constant source of food.

6. You can add a sophisticated edge to any planting scheme by using trained fruit – this can include stepover apples, espalier pears and apples, and fan-trained cherries and redcurrants.

GO GREENER

In the autumn, let some of the vegetables, including onions and radishes, go to seed. This adds winter interest and seed for the coming year.

Lettuce and chard have a variety of leaf colours

Constructing crazy containers

This is the container equivalent of crazy paving, but with a
great deal of added colour. Think 'pop art' when it comes to
containers – use all shapes and sizes, planted up with a selection
of tropical plants with colourful leaves and flowers to lift your
spirits. Just remember to dig drainage holes where necessary.

Elements to consider

Space You'll want a spot that is sunny for most
of the day, though some partial shade will also
work. It should be sheltered from the wind and
not in a rain shadow. These are thirsty plants,
and it makes sense to be near a water butt.

You can tailor the plants to your space, but
if you are going tropical with the likes of
banana, you'll need some extra room as their
leaves can be a few metres long.

Containers Go crazy with old pots of all sizes
and paint them rainbow colours. Or create some
'pop art' on old rubbish bins or other containers
from a reclamation yard. The more brash and
bold the look, the better.

Make sure at least one of your containers has
enough depth for large-leaved tropical plants.

*Cabinet curiosity: this drawer crammed with succulents
contains many different textures and colours.*

Tea leaves: a teapot and mug turn out to be just the place for a green planting combination.

Soil, drainage and care Soil should be fertile and rich, but not apt to get either waterlogged or too dry. Use loam-based with added grit (30 per cent). Dig in compost or well-rotted manure. The grit in the soil will aid drainage. Place crocks at the bottom.

Use a natural feed such as seaweed or comfrey regularly during the growing season.

Design and plant choice Borrow from the classic container design book: think 'thriller, filler, spiller' and then double it. Having several containers grouped together means you can allow room for a banana tree or a tree fern as a major focal point, but with neighbouring containers for colourful cannas and showy dahlias.

Look also for plants with showstopper leaves such as coleus or dark aeoniums.

Exotic plants to try

Banana The classic banana (*Musa basjoo*), or the smaller pink banana *(Musa velutina)*, which is more colourful.

Tree ferns and palms Evergreen choices include the windmill palm and fan palms. Australian tree ferns have chunky trunks and huge finely cut leaves.

Colourful Bird of paradise, pineapple and ginger lilies, fuchsias, cannas and hot dahlias in bright oranges, reds and hot pink.

Stunning leaves Coleus come in wild colour combos and the heart-shaped leaves of *Caladium* will light up an understorey (they like shade). Dark aeoniums provide exotic contrast.

Green appeal *Fatsia japonica* has architectural leaves, white flowers and black fruit.

Winter wonder

A winter container can be elegant with ferns and winter white, or colourful with pops of red and pink. You can tailor it to reflect a celebration: Christmas, Diwali, Hanukkah or even the winter solstice. Add lights for nighttime sparkle.

TIP

Evergreen shrubs like yew, privet or holly provide a variety of textures and shapes to add interest in winter. Avoid box, as it is prone to too many problems.

Elements to consider

Location Place where it can get as much of the winter sun as possible. You could locate them by a front door or on the porch, where it is easy to spot, or outside a window that you often look out of.

Containers Any container should be frost-resistant and large enough to accommodate three or more plants; if space is an issue, a single shrub or small tree with underplanting will do the trick.

Make this a permanent planting, refreshed with plants as necessary yearly, and think long term when choosing a container.

Soil and care Use a peat-free compost and raise the container off the ground on 'pot feet' (or bricks) to prevent the pot from standing in water that may cause roots to rot or pots to crack. There is no need to feed, even for winter flowering plants, but make sure it doesn't dry out. If it snows, give your plants a shake so they don't break or bow.

Plants Plants will not grow much, if at all, in the winter, so make sure they are the right size. There is a wide variety of dwarf conifers, so double-check before you buy to make sure it will stay small. Pair this with variegated ivy, cyclamen or pansies. Underplant bay and holly 'lollipop' or triangle shapes with bee-friendly crocus and snowdrops.

Larger containers could feature a dwarf cypress or a young white birch contrasted with red cornus stems and ivy underplanting. Berries and rosehips look festive and birds love them.

Plants to try

Winter berries Ivy, holly, hawthorn and dog rose.

Shrubs Skimmia, rosemary, sage, winter heather and prickly heath (*Gaultheria mucronata*).

Dwarf conifers Juniper 'Compressa', *Pinus mugo* 'Mops' and *Picea glauca* 'Conica'.

Evergreen Bay, box, ivy and yew.

Winter climbers Winter jasmine and winter honeysuckle.

Bee-friendly Pansies, hellebores, crocus and snowdrops.

Grasses and sedges *Carex*, hardy fountain grass and pheasant's tail grass.

Frosty Dusty Miller, silver fern (*Athyrium niponicum* 'Metallicum') and curry plant.

*Above: The bright yellow flowers that appear on the bare branches of winter jasmine (*Jasminum nudiflorum*) can brighten up a bleak container garden in the winter.*

Dry crevice garden

A crevice garden cannot help being a dramatic focal point – there is something so rugged about the way it mimics a mountain environment, its jagged rocks placed sideways, its fissures perfect for hardy plants.

Elements to consider

Space Choose a sunny and open spot. Size doesn't matter as long as it looks balanced. A small trough or bowl can still look rugged and intriguing if the rocks are large enough to be the focus of attention. For maximum impact, go for a larger trough that can accommodate a dozen or so pieces of jagged rock.

Containers It is traditional to use a stone trough or sink, but you can also make your own using an old washing-up bowl or even a cardboard box by mixing up some hypertufa.

You can use greener alternatives of coir fibre and sand rather than the conventional peat moss and perlite. Greener cement options are harder to find but include lime which, for instance, can be mixed with hemp hurd to make hempcrete.

Rocks There is no 'right' sort of rock to use – the point is to look uneven and rugged. Soil needs to be mounded up before the rocks go in. The classic look is slabs of flat rock of varying size and shape arranged close to each other. Stick to one type of rock and bury them at least half underground.

GO GREENER

Darker rocks absorb more heat than lighter colours, which will either warm or cool the soil. If your climate is cooler, you may want to go darker.

Drainage, soil and care Drainage is essential for succulents and alpines, so make sure there are enough holes in your container bottom. A screen or crocks/gravel will stop soil escaping. Use free-draining soil – you can make your own.

One recipe to try is roughly half and half sand or grit and (peat-free) soil. Remove dead foliage to avoid rot and don't over-fertilize.

Plants Small really is beautiful when it comes to saxatiles – plants that live among rocks. A crevice garden is all about the rhizosphere – where the roots live. Even a small trough will have different microclimates and the roots of plants at soil level will receive more water than those growing between the rocks higher up. Remember that chasmophytes – 'abyss dwellers' – are plants that like to live in crevice spaces where they face almost no competition from other plants.

Plants to try

Succulents Delosperma, crimson stonecrop (*Sedum spurium* 'Dragon's Blood'), *Lewisia cotyledon,* hen and chickens (or houseleeks) (*Sempervivum*).

Classics Cyclamens, rock pinks, small bellflowers (*Campanula*) and rockfoils (*Saxifraga*).

Old friends Aubretia, aurinia, alyssum, *Phlox subulata,* alpine asters, sea thrift and creeping thyme.

Star-shaped white flowers Edelweiss.

Stone trough crevice garden

This crevice garden brings a little bit of mountain magic to a sunny patio, with alpines and succulents clinging to the cracks. It's pretty and practical – dry gardens are a good fit with climate change and work well in a world where water is scarcer.

Plants between the rocks, like this crocus, will have extra root room

Planning a crevice garden

1. Rocks should be jagged and ragged, half-submerged in your container – place them closely together with a gap of 2.5cm (1in), at an angle to the trough or container. Don't be afraid to go high – that's what gives mountains their drama.

2. Alpines and succulents are all about small curves; they grow in cushions, buns, tufts and carpets. Use multiples of one plant, so they will bloom together, and space them out, unevenly, as is nature's way.

3. The mix here includes early-flowering crocus and dwarf tulips *(Tulipa sogdiana)* as well as cyclamen for later in the season. Most dry garden plants flower in summer and these add early- and late-season interest, as well as nectar for bees.

4. Place your crevice container near a seating area to get up close and personal with the vibrant jewel-box colours of many alpines, raised closer to the eye by the extra height of the rocks.

5. Crevice gardens are not for the impatient, as alpine and succulent plants tend to be slow growing and long-lived.

6. Just because it is a 'dry' garden doesn't mean it doesn't need rain or, in the case of prolonged dry spells, watering. Hand-water with a watering can outfitted with a fine rose – the goal is to mimic rain, allowing it to trickle through the crevices.

Graduated higher rocks add drama and interest

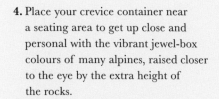

GO GREENER

It was common to see houseleeks growing on roofs as, for centuries, it has been seen as a magical plant that could protect your home from lightning as well as from witches.

Setting up a rain garden

A rain garden – also called a Sustainable Drainage System or SuDS – container is a brilliant way to get the most of every drop of rain. It absorbs water that otherwise would run off hard surfaces and, planted up with flowerful perennials and grasses, provides a wildlife habitat to boot.

Elements to consider

Location Locate your containers underneath a rain chain or drainpipe or next to (or linked via a longer hose or pipe) a water butt.

It should not drain directly into ground near a wall or building, so direct any overflow away or into an existing drain.

Varying container heights creates a soothing water soundscape

Be sure to test your containers to make sure they are watertight

Rain gardens can be container ponds or, as is more usual, filled with soil and plants that can adapt to being waterlogged for short periods

Containers There is no 'right' way to build a rain garden, though it should not be too small or it will flood. The idea is to have one planted in a container, raised up on bricks, that absorbs any rainfall initially. The drainage hole (fitted with a hose or pipe) is usually on one side for overflow, which escapes either directly down into another container or is taken away, via a rill or pipe.

You can buy a bespoke rain garden container or make your own. You can experiment with old plastic storage boxes and washing-up bowls placed on bricks at various heights, and disguised behind a framework of bricks, wood or stone.

Plants Rain gardens need plants that can cope with being waterlogged for up to 48 hours but can also withstand dry periods. Grasses and sedges should be part of the mix, providing structure in winter, and a habitat for insects.

Pioneer SuDS borders (such as the Grey to Green scheme in Sheffield) have used a wide mix of plants (grasses, euphorbias, asters, rudbeckias, rosemary, echinacea, and so on) to create colourful bee-friendly beds.

Soil and care Soil should be low-nutrient and include at least 30 per cent grit and sand. The bottom should have a good layer of gravel (at least 10cm; 4in). The plants should require no feeding or, in general, watering. Deadhead and cut back as necessary.

Plants to try

Shrubs Elderflower, cornus (including the fiery stemmed 'Midwinter Fire'), hydrangeas, rosemary and *Rosa rugosa*.

Perennials Bugle, *Geranium* 'Rozanne', *Iris sibirica*, *Crocosmia* 'Lucifer', euphorbias, rudbeckia, daisies and asters.

Grasses Korean feather reed grass (*Calamagrostis brachytricha*), *Carex secta*, tufted hair grass (*Deschampsia cespitosa*) and silver grass (*Miscanthus sinensis*).

GO GREENER

A rain chain dangling over a tropical container planting will help make sure that it gets as much water as possible.

Pond in a pot

An aquatic container – or a 'pond in a pot' – is a game-changer for your garden, attracting dragonflies and damselflies, as well as frogs and toads. Water brings movement and dancing light to any space.

Elements to consider

Location Look for a spot that enjoys the sun for only part of the day, as it could overheat in summer. Place it near other greenery to attract wildlife. Give your container a 'dry run' to make sure it works – once filled, moving it can become quite the project.

GO GREENER

Set up your aquatic container (without plants) over the winter so it can be in place to fill up with springtime showers.

A container pond will attract all types of wildlife including inquisitive and thirsty birds.

Containers Anything goes as long as it is watertight, or you can make it so. A butler's sink or a recycled metal bucket will work in a small space; but a larger container, such as an old metal trough, will allow more room for interesting plant combinations.

Compost and planting Use rainwater instead of tap water if possible, as plants much prefer it. Use medium to heavy loam; garden soil will work but only if free from fertilizer and herbicides – otherwise, buy aquatic compost.

Position plants in latticed baskets, filled about halfway with compost. A lining of hessian fabric (or recycled plastic) will stop soil escaping, and pebbles or gravel on top will ensure nothing floats away. Use rocks or bricks to create 'steps' for planting marginals and to create ladders for frogs to enter and exit.

Wildlife Water beetles, dragonflies, damselflies, caddisfly larvae and water striders will be drawn to water and aquatic plants. Frogs and newts are common in garden ponds – they eat slugs and snails, as well as many insects. A pond can also be a drinking station for birds and bats.

Plants Choose plants that like a variety of depths (create underwater shelves with bricks or stones). Place marginals or bog plants 5–15cm (2–6in) below the surface. Put deep marginals up to 40cm (16in) below the surface and include taller varieties such as rushes. Submerged plants, such as waterlilies, rest on the bottom.

Within any mix, include a 'submerged floater' oxygenating weed such as hornwort.

Plants to try

Marginals Marsh marigold, water forget-me-not and watercress.

Deep marginals Water mint, Iris versicolor, water plantain and pickerelweed.

Grasses and rushes Dwarf horsetail, flowering rush and cotton grass.

⊙ **Waterlilies** *Nymphaea alba* (for larger ponds); miniatures: 'Helvola' (yellow), 'Rubra' (red); dwarfs: 'Paul Hariot' (yellow), 'Perry's Baby Red' and 'Xiatei' (pink).

Oxygenators Hornwort, milfoil and crowfoot.

Garden in a metal trough

This trough, which is placed at the side of a patio in dappled shade for some of the day, contains a pretty combination of aquatic plants and will be a 'destination visit' for all sorts of wildlife.

Creating a trough garden

1. Waterlilies are pond superstars – but make sure their size reflects their home. Large containers may be able to accommodate the UK native waterlily *Nymphaea alba*. For smaller ponds (80cm; 32in across) use dwarf varieties, and for those 60cm (24in) wide use miniatures (pygmaea). Remember: waterlilies like sun and don't like to be splashed.

Surface aquatic plants include delicious watercress

GO GREENER

Frogs will munch on snails and slugs as well as more than 100 insects in just one night.

2. When designing an aquatic container, think colour, season, height, shape – with an added dimension in terms of planting depths. Bricks and rocks create underwater shelves for shallow and deep marginals; add a waterlily or floating plant, and at least one tall grass or rush to provide height and balance.

3. A pond attracts bees, hoverflies, water skaters and dragonflies. To bring frogs to your pond, choose a container that is not too high and make a ladder (stones or rocks work well) to help them in and out. They will appreciate a spot with shady leaves to hide under.

4. Many aquatic plants are edible, including water mint and waterlily roots, but the best known is watercress. It's an easy-to-grow marginal that likes to be on the highest shelf, just below the water level. It likes running water but also grows well in a still pond.

5. All ponds need oxygenators, such as hornwort – shy plants that live below the surface and help keep the water fresh. They use dissolved mineral salts from the water and, by competing with algae for nutrients, also help limit its growth. They should only occupy about 30 per cent of the water.

6. Dragonflies are especially welcome visitors. To create a dragonfly habitat, provide upright plants, such as flowering rush or pickerelweed, for larvae to climb up and out of the water into dry conditions, so they can open their wings as adults.

Reeds and grasses add height and movement

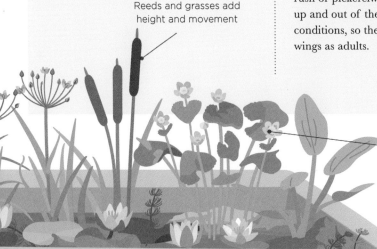

Plan so that at least one plant is in flower

ECO WORRIER

Refrain from having fish in your garden pond as they can pollute the water and eat the likes of frogspawn and tadpoles.

Weeds on show

The idea of creating an attractive container full of what are commonly seen as weeds or, as some are now calling them, 'weed heroes' or 'superweeds', is an intriguing prospect. Wildlife will love it, and expect some surprised – and impressed – comments from human visitors, too.

Dandelions are key plants for attracting wildlife including birds, bees, butterflies and moths.

Elements to consider

Location This will depend on what you plan to grow and the purpose of your display. There are superweeds that grow in sun or shade and all things in between.

If your display is for practical purposes and features stinging nettles (for making a fertilizer), you may want to place it out of reach.

Containers A larger container, or a group of three varying sizes, will be enough to create a 'wild patch' habitat/microclimate – but the right mix of plants in a smaller container, such as a window box, will still bring in bees and butterflies.

Soil and care This is the ultimate low-maintenance container garden. Soil should be low-nutrient and include grit or sand. They will require no feeding or care, though you could, if you wanted, deadhead and cut back as you think necessary.

Plants 'Weed out' those you do not want. The likes of couch grass or cleavers may not be on your list. Ragweed will not appeal to the allergic. You might reject some because you don't want them spreading into your main garden – the bright pink rosebay willowherb could look stunning in a container, but its seeds spread easily.

Many 'weed heroes' attract certain types of wildlife (for example, garlic mustard and orange-tip butterflies), so you may choose them for that reason. You may want to also consider weed 'cultivars', such as blood dock.

GO GREENER

Create a 'nest' or small log pile of twigs and branches in your container to provide overwintering habitat for some insects and bees.

Plants to try

Ground cover Creeping buttercup, lesser celandine, common daisy and dandelion.

Midrange Herb robert, green alkanet, garlic mustard, cow parsley, knapweed, stinging nettles, white deadnettle and clover.

Tall Meadowsweet, hogweed, ragwort, mullein, teasel and wild angelica.

Climbers Bindweed, blackberry and vetch.

Wildflower 'weeds' Road verge regulars include wild marjoram, cranesbill (*Geranium pratense*) and dog rose.

◉ Disused railway pioneers Buddleja and rosebay willowherb.

Plants to grow

This is your guide to a cornucopia of plants
that work particularly well in container gardens.
The choice ranges from little to large, from the
smallest flower to trees and shrubs. There are
flowers, fruit and vegetables, ferns, grasses, bulbs,
aquatics, alpines, herbs, climbers and, yes, weeds.
We have also listed wildlife and other eco-friendly
considerations for each. You will find some old
favourites here and some new ones that could
become treasured discoveries.

RHS HARDINESS SCALE

Rating	Temperature ranges °C	Category
H1	5 to 15°C and above	tropical, subtropical and warm temperate
H2	1 to 5°C	tender
H3	1 to –5°C	half hardy
H4	–10 to –5°C	hardy for an average UK winter
H5	–15 to –10°C	hardy in a cold winter
H6	–20 to –15°C	hardy in a very cold winter
H7	–20 and below	very hardy

Plants to grow: Tree profiles

Trees add impact and drama to any container setting and also bring many ecological benefits in terms of carbon saving and providing wildlife habitats. When choosing a tree, look for multi-season interest and, when it comes to container gardening, it is important to look for a variety that will not grow too tall too quickly.

TIP

Any entries marked with the star plant icon are container superstars that offer multi-tasking appeal

STAR PLANT

Hazel
Corylus avellana

Sun: Full sun/partial shade
Soil type: Chalk, loam, sand
Height: 4-8m (13-26ft)
(5-10 years to reach full height)
Spread: 4-8m (13-26ft)
Hardiness: H6
Thrives: Temperate zones, native of Europe, also now in parts of North America
Wildlife: Moths, caterpillars, dormice, birds

It is a sure sign that spring is around the corner when you see the long, yellow catkins dangling from the bare branches of hazel. This deciduous tree is grown for coppicing and is a wildlife hero. Its downy leaves are favoured by caterpillars and moths, early flying bees collect pollen from the male catkins and the small nuts produced in the autumn are eaten by dormice as well as many birds – and are also tasty for humans. 'Contorta' (shown opposite) is a popular form with twisted branches.

Hawthorn

Crataegus monogyna

Sun: Full sun/partial shade
Soil type: All
Height: 4–8m (13–26ft)
(20-plus years to reach full height)
Spread: 4–8m (13–26ft)
Hardiness: H7
Thrives: Temperate zones, UK, Europe, North Africa, southwest Asia
Wildlife: Birds, bees, moths, insects

⊙ This deciduous UK native is also known as the May tree, which refers to the scented white flowers that emerge in that month, signalling the shift from spring to summer. It has deep red haws that form in the autumn, which can be used to make jellies and jams, and are rich in antioxidants. Its dense foliage is beloved by birds and dormice, and it can support more than 300 species of insects – including various caterpillars of moths.

Paperbark maple

Acer griseum

Sun: Full sun/partial shade
Soil type: All
Height: 8–12m (26–39ft)
(20-plus years to reach full height)
Spread: 4–8m (13–26ft)
Hardiness: H5
Thrives: China, UK, Europe, North America
Wildlife: Birds, pollinators

⊙ This deciduous tree is renowned for the beauty of its constantly peeling papery bark, which changes colour from chestnut to cinnamon, the ruffly curls remaining on the tree throughout the year, even during winter. This outstanding ornamental tree also has brilliant red and orange autumn colour. It is small and spreading, and ideal as a focal point near a seating area. The tree is beneficial to wildlife, but would benefit from being underplanted with pollinator plants.

Rowan

Sorbus aucuparia

Sun: Full sun/partial shade
Soil type: Loam and sand
Height: 12m-plus (39ft-plus)
(20-50 years to reach full height)
Spread: 4-8m (13-26ft)
Hardiness: H6
Thrives: UK, Europe, North America, Russia, central and northern Asia
Wildlife: Bees, caterpillars, birds

Often found in the countryside but, tolerant of pollution, the rowan is a UK native and is widely planted as a street and city garden tree. It has white flowers in the spring and autumn colour as well as orange-red berries – though other varieties have pink or white berries. Bees love the flowers, caterpillars feast on the leaves and many types of bird eat the berries (which also make an excellent jam).

Crab apple

Malus sylvestris

Sun: Full sun/partial shade
Soil type: All
Height: 8-12m-plus (26-39ft-plus)
(20-50 years to reach full height)
Spread: 4-8m (13-26ft)
Hardiness: H6
Thrives: Temperate zones, Europe, South America, Australia
Wildlife: Bees, caterpillars, birds

These small and rounded deciduous trees are one of the ancestors of the cultivated apple and can grow to become 'crabbed' and twisted in appearance. They flower in early spring (white scented blooms), which later turn into small yellow-green fruit that can be made into a jelly. They are a boon to wildlife of all types and birds and mammals such as mice, voles and foxes eat the fruit.

Birch

Betula

Sun: Full sun/partial shade
Soil type: All
Height: Varies according to variety
Spread: 4-8m (13-26ft)
Hardiness: H7
Thrives: Temperate zones, Himalayas, UK, Europe, Asia, North America
Wildlife: Insects, caterpillars

⬇ The elegant silver birch has enjoyed a bout of popularity in recent years for urban planting, but for containers, be sure to source a smaller version than the UK native *Betula pendula*. One smaller variety, *Betula utilis* 'Doorenbos' is particularly sought after for its white exfoliating bark and slender form. Its graceful look, however, masks a tough tree – it grows in all soils and conditions. It has catkins in the spring and autumn colour with winter interest provided by the bark (the sap can be used to make beer). It provides food for insects and caterpillars.

Plants to grow: Edimental profiles

Edibles that are also ornamentals – or 'edimentals' – have a splendid combination of pluses to them. The fruit and vegetables, as well as patio orchard trees, look (and taste) scrumptious, are useful for wildlife and will save you money and food miles.

STAR PLANT

Rainbow chard
Beta vulgaris subsp. *cicla* var. *flavescens*

Sun: Full sun/partial shade
Soil type: All
Height: Up to 60cm (24in)
Spread: Up to 40cm (16in)
Hardiness: H6
Thrives: Widely adaptable worldwide
Wildlife: Caterpillars
Care: Sow in early spring

Rainbow chard is a stunning ornamental with vibrant purple, yellow and red stalks and lush green leaves. It has the 'wow factor' and fits in particularly well in tropical-style container plantings. It has an ancient history, a cultivated descendant of the wild sea beet that was supposedly grown in the Hanging Gardens of Babylon and ancient Rome. It is easy to grow, with seeds sown in early spring to midsummer, with leaves ready for picking in 10 to 12 weeks. You'll need to patrol for slugs.

Strawberry

Fragaria x *ananassa* 'Cambridge Favourite'

Sun: Full sun
Soil type: Fertile, well-drained
Height: 10-50cm (4-20in)
Spread: 10-50cm (4-20in)
Hardiness: H6
Thrives: Grown worldwide
Wildlife: Bees
Care: Plant in spring or early autumn

● There are hundreds of strawberry varieties, but they all fall into three general categories: summer-fruiting, ever-bearing or wild/alpine. All three make excellent container plants, and the fruit can look especially attractive trailing down from the edge (thus, also avoiding resting on soil where they can mould). 'Cambridge Favourite' is disease resistant – an important attribute when choosing. Bees love the flowers and birds will zoom in on berries, so don't tarry if you want to harvest.

Black kale

Brassica aleracea 'Nero di Toscana'

Sun: Full sun/partial shade
Soil type: All
Height: 90cm (35in)
Spread: 60cm (24in)
Hardiness: H7
Thrives: Grown worldwide, originally from Tuscany
Wildlife: Insects, caterpillars
Care: Remove caterpillars

● Black kale manages to be delicious, attractive and full of antioxidants. It is an excellent 'backdrop' plant, with green-black leaves providing a stunning contrast for other plants and flowers. The narrow leaves can be picked from late summer to early spring and have a lighter flavour to regular kale. Plant with nasturtiums, which attract caterpillars and aphids and can act as a sacrifice or 'trap' crop.

Lettuce

Lactuca sativa

Sun: Full sun/partial shade
Soil type: Humus-rich
Height: 30cm (12in)
Spread: 30cm (12in)
Hardiness: H3
Thrives: Grown worldwide
Wildlife: Caterpillars and slugs
Care: Remove slugs

The motto for growing leaf lettuce is 'little and often'; sow a limited number of seeds every 14 days or so and enjoy fresh leaves all summer long. They look great in containers, especially if you include a red-leaved variety. You can make your own 'cut and come again' mix that includes spinach, rocket and mustard, or buy a packet of mixed seeds. Weed carefully and go on nighttime patrol for slugs.

Cherry tomato

Solanum lycopersicum 'Tumbling Tom'

Sun: Full sun
Soil type: Humus-rich
Height: 50cm (20in)
Spread: 50cm (20in)
Hardiness: H3
Thrives: Grown worldwide, originally from South America
Wildlife: Bees
Care: Water and feed regularly

This is a busy compact cultivar that looks great in containers of any size. Plant among flowering perennials or with herbs in a window box, where its fruit can trail down over the edge. Another plus for 'Tumbling Tom' is that it does not require training. It is easy to grow and the abundant small, sweet fruit is delicious. Sow midwinter to early spring and harvest late summer to early autumn. Be vigilant in watering and feeding.

Broad bean

Vicia faba 'Crimson Flowered'

Sun: Full sun/partial shade
Soil type: Fertile, well-drained
Height: Up to 90cm (35in)
Spread: 10-45cm (4-18in)
Hardiness: H6
Thrives: North and South America, Europe, Africa, China
Wildlife: Bees
Care: Pinch out growing tips to avoid blackfly

◐ All types of bean – including French, runner and broad – make for attractive edimentals, with bee-friendly summer flowers that turn into hanging pods. The heritage varieties hold a particular charm, and this broad bean is especially pretty with its deep crimson flowers that develop into short pods. It likes a sunny warm spot and is easy to grow, producing an early crop of tender beans.

Discovery apple

Malus domestica 'Discovery'

Sun: Full sun
Soil type: Chalk, sand, clay
Height: 2.5m–3m (8–10ft) (M26 rootstock)
Spread: 2.5m (8ft)
Hardiness: H6
Thrives: Temperate zones, UK cultivar, species grown worldwide except Africa
Wildlife: Bees, birds
Care: Pruning is essential

➊ 'Discovery' apples are crisp and sweet. They look splendid on the tree as they ripen, and are ready to be picked for eating as early as late summer. The type was discovered in Essex in 1949, by a fruit farm worker who planted some pips of 'Worcester Pearmain', a 19th century variety. It is in pollination group 3 and attracts bees. Apples have had a wicked reputation as a 'forbidden fruit' right from the start, as Eve just couldn't resist it.

Victoria plum

Prunus domestica 'Victoria'

Sun: Full sun
Soil type: All
Height: Up to 3.5m (12ft) (St Julian A)
Spread: Up to 3m (10ft)
Hardiness: H5
Thrives: Temperate zones, UK cultivar, species grown worldwide
Wildlife: Bees, butterflies, moths, birds, small mammals
Care: Thinning required

➊ This long-term favourite is self-fertile and produces sweet reddish-purple fruit with golden flesh. Use it for cooking, canning, bottling or just eating. It needs to be thinned to avoid biennial fruiting. In containers, it may not fruit for two to three years. Named after Queen Victoria, it has been cultivated in England since 1847. It is a food source for many butterflies and moths and a favourite of bees.

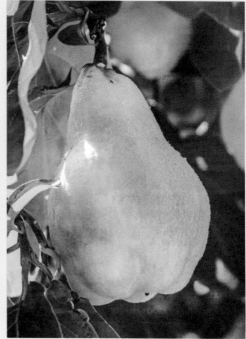

Blueberry
Vaccinium 'Northcountry'

Sun: Full sun/partial shade
Soil type: Sand, clay
Height: 50cm–1m (20in–3ft)
Spread: 50cm–1m (20in–3ft)
Hardiness: H7
Thrives: Temperate zones, North America,
Mexico, Europe, South America
Wildlife: Bees, birds
Care: Yearly ericaceous mulch

⊕ Blueberries are often called a superfruit, and
the shrub also delivers in terms of appearance,
with white flowers in spring and dark green
leaves that turn a brilliant scarlet in autumn.
This is a half-high bush variety, suited for colder
climates and containers, but most other varieties
are suitable for container growing. It needs
acidic soil, with a pH 5.5 or lower. A yearly
ericaceous mulch of chopped-up pine needles
from the Christmas tree works well.

Quince
Cydonia oblonga 'Sibley's Patio Quince'

Sun: Full sun
Soil type: Sand, chalk
Height: 50cm–1m (20in–3ft)
Spread: 50cm–1m (20in–3ft)
Hardiness: H5
Thrives: Temperate zones, originally from
western Asia
Wildlife: Bees, birds
Care: Protect from rabbits

⊕ This is a grafted variety of a very small
tree that produces large and highly fragrant
yellow fruit that ripen in late autumn, making
for a great late-season harvest. Use cooked
for desserts or make into jelly or a paste called
membrillo, and serve with cheese and meats.
This patio variety has pink-white flowers
in spring and leaves that turn yellow in
autumn. This ancient fruit was a sacred
emblem of Aphrodite, the Greek goddess
of love and beauty.

Plants to grow: Shrub profiles

Shrubs are the gift that keeps on giving when it comes to containers – year after year these woody perennials continue to provide structure and colour. They are long-lasting and carbon saving. They can be used as a 'backdrop', their leaves setting off other flowers, or they can be stars in themselves. Many have flowers that attract wildlife, particularly bees and butterflies.

STAR PLANT

Elderflower
Sambucus nigra f. *porphyrophylla* 'Eva'

Sun: Full sun/partial shade
Soil type: All
Height: 2–3m (7–10ft)
Spread: 2m (7ft)
Hardiness: H7
Thrives: Widespread in Europe and temperate zones worldwide in specific areas
Wildlife: Bees, moths, butterflies, birds, small mammals
Care: Can be lightly pruned in late winter/early spring

⊖ The elderflower is a hedgerow stalwart, but this black variety is particularly striking with its dark dissected foliage that provides contrast to other plants. In late spring and early summer, it becomes a showstopper with large, flat, pale pink umbels (lightly scented) that are adored by moths and butterflies. In the autumn, the flowers transform into small blackish-red berries that attract birds and can be eaten by small mammals such as voles. For the best dark leaf colour, place in full sun.

Dwarf buddleja
Buddleja davidii Buzz Series

Sun: Full sun/partial shade
Soil type: All
Height: 1.5-2.5m (5-8ft)
Spread: 50cm-1m (20in-3ft)
Hardiness: H7
Thrives: Worldwide, native of China
Wildlife: Butterflies, moths
Care: Cut back to one or two buds in early spring

☉ Buddlejas, introduced from China in the 1890s, are so easy to grow that they are now ubiquitous. The Buzz Series is one of several dwarf varieties that suits containers and will provide a summer of abundant conical flowers that, depending on variety, can be white, pink, lavender or darker purple. Buddleja is called the 'butterfly bush' and is one of the UK's top nectar shrubs, attracting a wide variety of butterflies. It can get leggy if not cut back in early spring.

Smoke bush
Cotinus coggygria

Sun: Full sun/partial shade
Soil type: All
Height: Dwarf 1-1.5m (3-5ft), otherwise up to 4m (13ft)
Spread: 50cm-1m (20in-3ft)
Hardiness: H5
Thrives: Europe, North America, Asia, native of China
Wildlife: Bees
Care: Prune hard in early spring

☉ The smoke bush has dark reddish-purple leaves in the summer that, in autumn, become vibrant reds, oranges and yellows. In the summer, its large flowers – which attract bees and other pollinators – transform into what looks like clouds of pink smoke. For a container, choose a dwarf variety or keep smaller by annual pruning. For best leaf colour, choose a sunny spot. There are varieties with acid-green leaves that tolerate shade better.

Hydrangea
Hydrangea 'Runaway Bride'

Sun: Full sun/partial shade
Soil type: All
Height: Up to 1.2m (4ft)
Spread: Up to 1.2m (4ft)
Hardiness: H6
Thrives: Temperate zones, native of Japan
Wildlife: Pollinators
Care: Mulch to help keep soil moist

Newer varieties of hydrangea come in a large number of different types of flowers and colours, many of which are suitable for containers. Be aware that soil pH affects colour, with more acid soils producing blue petals and alkaline favouring the pinks. Hydrangeas flower from June to September and the variety 'Runaway Bride', an RHS Chelsea Plant of the Year, has particularly abundant blooms, as it is a garland hydrangea, producing white lacecap flowers along the length of its stems. Hydrangeas can attract pollinators and the flowers, which turn brown in late autumn, look attractive throughout winter.

Rosemary
Salvia rosmarinus 'Miss Jessopp's Upright'

Sun: Full sun
Soil type: All
Height: Up to 1m (3ft)
Spread: Up to 1m (3ft)
Hardiness: H4
Thrives: Temperate zones, native of Europe and North Africa
Wildlife: Bees and other insects
Care: Drought resistant

Rosemary is an all-rounder in terms of colour, form and use. It has delicate small pale blue flowers and dark green needle-like aromatic leaves. This is an upright evergreen that, in colder locations, will need winter protection.

It likes poor well-drained soil and adds culinary interest, as its leaves can be used to flavour roasting meats and vegetables. It can also be used to flavour vinegar, oils, butter, and so on.

Bay
Laurus nobilis

Sun: Full sun/partial shade
Soil type: All
Height: Up to 10m (33ft) if not clipped
Spread: Variable
Hardiness: H4
Thrives: Subtropical biome, native of Mediterranean
Wildlife: Pollinators
Care: Low maintenance

⊙ If left to its own devices, bay will grow into a tree. For containers, it needs to be clipped; its natural shape is bushy, but it is often trimmed into more formal shapes such as pyramids and balls (as well as topiary). Its dark green leaves are aromatic and used in cooking. It is valued primarily for its ability for shaping, and not its flowers (small and yellow) or fruit (berries on female plants). It likes a sheltered spot and may need protection over winter.

Plants to grow: Perennial profiles

Perennials can be dramatic and are dependable, year after year, and also give your containers their own mini ecosystems along the way. They provide star power with colour and height, and all of these are also attractive to bees and other pollinators.

Salvia
Salvia 'Amistad'

Sun: Full sun/partial shade
Soil type: Loam, sand, clay
Height: Up to 1.5m (5ft)
Spread: 10–50cm (4–20in)
Hardiness: H3
Thrives: Cultivated worldwide, native of South America
Wildlife: Bees, butterflies
Care: Protect from winter cold and frost

This is a stunning container plant, upright with large, darkly purple tubular flowers that last from early summer until well into autumn. Salvias are plants of the future, drought resistant and adaptable to climate change. They look great in all types of planting schemes and especially tropical and cottage garden ones. Grow in a sunny sheltered spot and protect from winter cold and frost. They are loved by bees and other pollinators. There is a vast number of perennial sages – this hybrid is from Argentina and is known as the 'friendship sage' (*amistad* means friendship).

Yarrow

Achillea millefolium 'Terracotta'

Sun: Full sun
Soil type: Chalk, loam, sand
Height: 1–1.5m (3–5ft)
Spread: 10–50cm (4–20in)
Hardiness: H7
Thrives: Cultivated worldwide, temperate zones
Wildlife: Bees, butterflies
Care: Cut back in early spring

➲ This is a particularly attractive cultivar of the UK's native yarrow, with its feathery grey-green foliage and flat flowerheads that bees and other pollinators adore. It's a good cut-flower plant and 'nectar bar' natural, and its upright nature means that it will not be a 'blocker' in a container. Other colourful cultivars include 'Lilac Beauty' and 'Red Velvet', or try the native white in a 'weed' container.

Lavender

Lavandula angustifolia 'Hidcote'

Sun: Full sun
Soil type: Chalk, sand, clay
Height: 60cm (24in)
Spread: 75cm (30in)
Hardiness: H7
Thrives: Temperate zones, native of the Mediterranean
Wildlife: Bees, butterflies
Care: Trim after flowering

➲ This classic lavender, named after the Arts and Crafts style garden in Gloucester, is a compact form of English lavender. It has spikes of scented and deep violet flowers and aromatic silvery-grey leaves. It's a container 'hero' that, in a mixed planting, can be positioned near the edge, perfuming the air if you brush past it. Several plantings together in one container can also work well.

Dahlia

Dahlia 'Bishop of Llandaff'

Sun: Full sun
Soil type: All
Height: 50cm-1m (20in-3ft)
Spread: 10-50cm (4-20in)
Hardiness: H3
Thrives: Widely cultivated, native of Mexico and Central America
Wildlife: Bees, butterflies
Care: Cut back to ground in autumn before lifting tubers

☝ There are so many different types of dahlia – pompom, cactus, waterlily – but the 'Bishop of Llandaff' is an exceptional choice for containers. Its deep chocolate-black foliage provides a perfect contrast for flowers, including its own bright crimson blooms which last all summer (be sure to deadhead). Crucially, though, its flower structure – unlike so many dahlias – is relatively simple, which makes it very attractive to bees and butterflies. This dahlia looks very modern but won the RHS Award of Merit in 1928.

Helenium

Helenium 'Moerheim Beauty'

Sun: Full sun/partial shade
Soil type: All
Height: 50cm-1m (20in-3ft)
Spread: 10-30cm (4-12in)
Hardiness: H7
Thrives: Native of North and South America, also cultivated in Europe, Australia, Asia
Wildlife: Bees
Care: Cut back in winter

This coppery-red daisy – also known as sneezeweed – is beautiful as well as being fully hardy and easy to grow. It flowers from midsummer through to autumn, heating up plantings with its fiery hues. It has a dark, prominent centre that bees and other pollinators love. It can need staking (avoid windy positions anyway), but will be sturdier if given a Chelsea chop in late spring. It looks good with grasses.

Purpletop vervain

Verbena bonariensis

Sun: Sun
Soil type: All
Height: Up to 2m (7ft)
Spread: 30-40cm (12-16in)
Hardiness: H4
Thrives: Cultivated worldwide, native of South America
Wildlife: Bees
Care: Cut back in late autumn

This tall and airy perennial has sparse leaves and attractive flat heads of deep lavender flowers in summer and autumn that seem to float above other plants. It is a superb butterfly plant and adored by bees. It is elegant and practical, bringing height to a container without blocking it up. It works well with other perennials and grasses. The 'Lollipop' is a dwarf cultivar that grows to 60cm (24in).

Plants to grow: Annual profiles

Annual flowers have traditionally been seen as the flamboyant gobstoppers of the horticultural world: cheap and cheerful bloomers, whose job was to fill border gaps. It's time for a reappraisal – these annuals provide colour for your containers while also attracting masses of bees and butterflies. When choosing plants, remember that pollinators will avoid varieties that have double petals or are pollen-free.

STAR PLANT

Cornflower
Centaurea cyanus

Sun: Full sun
Soil type: Sand and clay
Height: 75cm (30in)
Spread: 10–50cm (4–20in)
Hardiness: H7
Thrives: Northern hemisphere, plus some parts of the southern hemisphere
Wildlife: Bees, butterflies
Care: Deadhead regularly

This easy-to-grow wildflower is thought to have been brought to Britain by Iron Age farmers some 2,400 years ago. For centuries, it was seen as a 'weed' of cornfields and was almost wiped out by widespread use of herbicides. It was named a 'Priority Species' in the UK Post-2010 Biodiversity Framework. Bees and butterflies love its bright blue flowers. It is regularly used in wildflower mixes and to add extra colour to borders; it can be grown in a range of colours. The buds are just as attractive as the edible flowers, which require regular deadheading.

Nasturtium

Tropaeolum majus

Sun: Full sun
Soil type: Loam, sand, clay
Height: Up to 2m (7ft)
Spread: 50cm-1m (20in-3ft)
Hardiness: H3
Thrives: Europe and North America, subtropical zones, native of Peru
Wildlife: Bees, butterflies, other pollinators
Care: Don't let them get too dry

☉ The garden nasturtium is a trailing climber, which flowers in the summer and autumn with abundant blooms ranging from orange to yellow and red. It comes in a range of shapes and sizes, including the more compact bush form (try the heirloom 'Empress of India', a bushy dwarf variety with vermillion blooms). Nasturtiums, which often self-seed, are easy to grow and you can sow seeds in situ outside. The flowers are edible and add a peppery taste to salads, and their seed pods can be used as capers.

Sunflower

Helianthus annuus

Sun: Full sun
Soil type: All
Height: 1.5m (5ft)
Spread: 50cm (20in)
Hardiness: H4
Thrives: Cultivated worldwide, native of southwestern US
Wildlife: Bees, butterflies
Care: Deadhead during summer

☉ There are more than 70 varieties of sunflower, but this tall bright yellow bloomer provides nectar for butterflies and bees, and seeds for us and the birds. Not everyone wants to grow a 'Vincent van Gogh' bouquet, and some dramatic colour choices include the deep maroon 'Claret' or the duo-coloured 'Ms Mars'. Deadhead during the summer, but towards autumn leave the seedheads for a dramatic winter silhouette.

Cosmos

Cosmos bipinnatus Apollo Series

Sun: Full sun
Soil type: All
Height: 65cm (26in)
Spread: 30cm (12in)
Hardiness: H3
Thrives: Cultivated worldwide, temperate zones, native of Mexico
Wildlife: Bees, butterflies
Care: Deadhead regularly

The cosmos flowers away happily throughout the summer into autumn. Its delicate blooms and feathery foliage allows it to look great while not becoming a 'bed blocker'. There is a wide variety of cosmos types and the 'Apollo Series' – a dwarf and compact variety that includes white, pink and carmine flowers – is particularly suited to container living. Cosmos looks particularly beautiful during a breezy day.

Tobacco plant

Nicotiana alata 'Lime Green'

Sun: Full sun/partial shade
Soil type: Chalk, loam, sand
Height: 60cm (24in)
Spread: 10-60cm (4-24in)
Hardiness: H2
Thrives: Europe, India, Asia, native of Brazil and Argentina
Wildlife: Butterflies, moths
Care: Deadhead regularly

❂ *Nicotiana* is an evergreen that has long stems of acid-green trumpet flowers that look great when placed near other more vibrant colours. It flowers throughout the summer and can continue into the autumn, though it will not tolerate frosty weather. This plant emits a lovely scent at night, which acts as a magnet for night-flying moths. Be aware that the shade-loving *Nicotiana sylvestris* is much taller and can grow up to 1.5m (3ft).

Marigold

Calendula officinalis 'Indian Prince'

Sun: Full sun/partial shade
Soil type: Loam, sand, clay
Height: 10-50cm (4-20in)
Spread: 10-50cm (4-20in)
Hardiness: H5
Thrives: Cultivated worldwide, native of Europe
Wildlife: Bees, butterflies
Care: Deadhead regularly

Marigolds are enjoying a revival of late with varieties such as 'Indian Prince' adding a bit more glamour than you get with some. They are valuable bee plants, though be sure to pick a variety with an open centre. Marigolds are edible and used to make dyes. They attract beneficial insects such as ladybirds and lacewings, and are companion plants for a variety of vegetables.

Plants to grow: Shade lover profiles

There is something especially restful about a shade-loving container, with its various hues of green and the flowers, mostly soft pastels. Some, such as the hellebores, come along just when you think winter will never end. Look for those with silvery or variegated leaves to add a shimmer of glamour to your containers.

STAR PLANT

Hard shield fern
Polystichum aculeatum

Sun: Partial/full shade
Soil type: Humus-rich
Height: 60cm (24in)
Spread: 90cm (35in)
Hardiness: H7
Thrives: Europe, northern Africa, Asia
Wildlife: Provides cover for insects, frogs
Care: Remove old leathery fronds in spring

⊖ This UK native fern is an evergreen but also refreshes itself in spring, its fronds unfurling backwards before settling into a shuttlecock shape. It looks good in smaller spaces, and is an elegant and graceful addition, no matter how shady it may be. It adds structure to container plantings and looks particularly good with hostas and hellebores. Plant in multiples for a lusher look. The hard shield fern is tough and easy to grow, and provides shelter for beetles, insects and frogs.

Hosta

Hosta 'Patriot'

Sun: Full sun/partial shade
Soil type: Chalk, sand, clay
Height: 50cm–1m (20in–3ft)
Spread: 50cm–1m (20in–3ft)
Hardiness: H7
Thrives: Northern hemisphere, native of China
Wildlife: Bees, butterflies
Care: Remove dead leaves

➲ Hostas are stunning foliage plants and 'Patriot' (also called the plantain lily) is particularly striking with its green and creamy white oval leaves. It will light up a shady planting and, in summer, there are tall spikes of lavender-coloured flowers. Hostas like sheltered positions and well-drained but moist soil. They are favourites of snails and slugs, so be vigilant in picking them off.

Hellebore

Helleborus x *hybridus*

Sun: Full sun/partial shade
Soil type: Chalk, loam, sand
Height: 10–50cm (4–20in)
Spread: 10–50cm (4–20in)
Hardiness: H7
Thrives: Temperate zones, native of Europe and Asia
Wildlife: Bees, butterflies
Care: Cut back old leaves in early winter

➲ This hellebore (known also as the Lenten rose) is a cheery and welcome addition to the garden with its pastel flowers that appear in late winter. The open-facing blooms with yellow centres vary in colour, often changing as the flowering season progresses. A semi-evergreen perennial, its leaves can be a skin irritant, so use gloves when handling. It works well as a container 'star' or as underplanting.

Hart's tongue fern

Asplenium scolopendrium

Sun: Partial shade
Soil type: All
Height: Up to 60cm (24in)
Spread: Up to 60cm (24in)
Hardiness: H7
Thrives: Europe, North America, North Africa, western Asia
Wildlife: Provides cover for frogs and toads
Care: Remove dead leaves

This eye-catching fern gets its name because it is thought to look like the tongue of a deer. It has a simple structure of glossy fronds with wavy edges and orange spores on the underside. Some varieties, such as 'Angustatum', have more ruffled edges. It grows in cracks and crannies of walls, as well as in woodland settings, and underplants well with spring bulbs.

Brunnera

Brunnera macrophylla 'Jack Frost'

Sun: Partial/full shade
Soil type: All
Height: 10–50cm (4–20in)
Spread: 10–50cm (4–20in)
Hardiness: H6
Thrives: Northern hemisphere, Australia
Wildlife: Bees
Care: Low maintenance

This perennial, also known as Siberian bugloss, has striking heart-shaped foliage that is silver-grey with green edges and veins. It adds interest to a shady container and, from early spring all the way to early summer, its small baby-blue flowers – which are similar to forget-me-nots – rise in clusters above the leaves. It has good ground cover and is extremely reliable, as it is not affected by slugs or snails. It is also disliked by deer and rabbits.

Anemone

Anemone x *hybrida* 'Honorine Jobert'

Sun: Sun/partial shade
Soil type: All
Height: 1–1.5m (3–5ft)
Spread: 50cm (20in)
Hardiness: H6
Thrives: Grown worldwide, French cultivar
Wildlife: Bees, other pollinators
Care: Cut back in late winter

☻ This tall, graceful perennial is a stalwart performer in late summer through autumn, producing masses of white flowers with large yellow centres. Its wiry branched stems means it won't block up your containers and allows sight of other plants. It looks particularly good with grasses and ferns. Anemones (also called windflowers) are native to many temperate areas. This cultivar was discovered in France in 1852 and certainly has the *oh là là* factor.

Plants to grow: Grass profiles

Grasses bring another dimension to containers, with their slender leaves that sway gracefully in the slightest breeze. They look particularly effective near perennials or in groups on their own. Grasses come in many colours and, in addition to providing movement and foliage contrast, their seedheads attract birds.

Feather grass
Stipa tenuissima

Sun: Full sun
Soil type: All
Height: 60cm (24in)
Spread: 30cm (12in)
Hardiness: H7
Thrives: Grown in most of the world except Asia, native of South America and southern North America
Wildlife: Insects
Care: Comb to remove dead foliage in spring

A beautiful semi-evergreen grass that is particularly valued for introducing movement into any planting scheme. The leaves and plumes start off pale green, turning blonde over the summer. In colder climates it can lose most of its leaves over winter, but fresh growth appears in spring. It pairs well as a contrast to most flowers, but it's the way in which it wafts and waves in the wind that makes it a standout container plant.

Blue fescue

Festuca glauca 'Elijah Blue'

Sun: Full sun/partial shade
Soil type: Loam, sand, clay
Height: Up to 30cm (12in)
Spread: Up to 25cm (10in)
Hardiness: H5
Thrives: Temperate zones, European native
Wildlife: Birds
Care: Drought tolerant; comb through
to remove dead foliage in early spring

◗ This grass, with its small mounds of steely
blue foliage, is an elegant container plant that
works well as both an edging plant or a gap-
filler. In the summer, it has small blue-green
flower plumes that turn golden brown. It's
drought tolerant and good for birds who like
the seeds and use it for nesting material. It
works well with blue/purple perennials and in
Mediterranean planting. The blue colouring
will be more intense if placed in full sun.

Japanese forest grass

Hakonechloa macra 'Aureola'

Sun: Full sun/partial shade
Soil type: All
Height: Up to 40cm (16in)
Spread: Up to 35cm (14in)
Hardiness: H7
Thrives: Native of Japan, grown in
temperate zones
Wildlife: Cover for small wildlife
Care: Cut back in early winter

◖ A compact and striking grass that forms
cascading clumps that look great as an edging
and as an underlayer to shrubs or trees. The
narrow arching leaves are striped yellow and
green and, if placed in full sun, can take on
a reddish hue. Slender flower spikes emerge in
late summer. It is deciduous and doesn't mind
partial shade.

Pheasant's tail grass
Anemanthele lessoniana

Sun: Full sun/partial shade
Soil type: All
Height: Up to 1m (3ft)
Spread: Up to 1m (3ft)
Hardiness: H4
Thrives: New Zealand native, temperate zones, also grown in northern hemisphere
Wildlife: Birds
Care: Comb through in early spring

This is a changeling grass that, in spring, forms a fountain-shaped clump of green leaves that develop yellow, red and orange spots and streaks. As autumn turns to winter, and the cold sets in, the colour can become more vivid. It has airy rose-tinted flowerheads in summer and autumn. It is not really known how it got its name, though the colours are reminiscent of those of the male pheasant. A semi-evergreen that self-seeds easily.

Quaking grass
Briza media

Sun: Full sun
Soil type: All
Height: 50cm–1m (20in–3ft)
Spread: 10–50cm (4–20in)
Hardiness: H7
Thrives: Grown worldwide, primarily in temperate zones
Wildlife: Birds
Care: Cut back in early spring

◉ This delicate grass is a common sight in summer flower meadows, with small heart-shaped flowerheads dangling from delicate stems. A native perennial, its seeds are a source of food for farmland birds including greenfinches, house sparrows and yellow hammers. It adds movement and delicacy to containers and, being well-behaved, won't try and take over.

Wavy hair grass
Deschampsia flexuosa

Sun: Full sun/partial shade
Soil type: All
Height: 30–50cm (12–20in)
Spread: 30–50cm (12–20in)
Hardiness: H6
Thrives: Grown worldwide, temperate zones
Wildlife: Birds, caterpillars
Care: Prune in early spring

This tuft-forming grass is an evergreen perennial and, when flowering in summer, forms a haze of shaking flowerheads. It is a boon to wildlife and is the food plant of the caterpillar of the wall brown butterfly (a priority species). It is compact and prefers acidic soils, often found in heath and moorland. A yellow-leaved form, 'Tatra Gold', looks especially good in containers.

Plants to grow: Bulb profiles

There are few sights as welcome as the emergence of a nodding white snowdrop in deep midwinter. Bulbs look particularly good in containers, which 'frame' them and allow for closer inspection. They are also a way to extend the flowering season for early and late pollinators. Choose 'organic' bulbs that have not been grown with chemical pesticides or fertilizers. Think about planting up a 'lasagne' pot with layers of bulbs that will come up sequentially in spring and/or summer (see page 169 for planting depths). This is a wonderful way to brighten up a spot and it will please pollinators too.

STAR PLANT

Snowdrop
Galanthus nivalis

Sun: Partial shade
Soil type: All
Height: Up to 15cm (6in)
Spread: Up to 10cm (4in)
Hardiness: H5
Thrives: Temperate zones, native of central and southern Europe
Wildlife: Bees, other pollinators
Care: Divide every year or two

☻ The UK's common snowdrop, honey-scented, with long, thin, grey-green leaves and nodding solitary white three-petal heads, is seen as the best variety for pollinators. It likes partial shade and works well as underplanting in a container. It flowers from midwinter – a very welcome sight for pollinators who have woken up early. Plant 'in the green' in late winter or dry in the autumn.

Grape hyacinth
Muscari arneniacum 'Valerie Finnis'

Sun: Full sun/partial shade
Soil type: All
Height: 20cm (8in)
Spread: 10cm (4in)
Hardiness: H6
Thrives: Widely cultivated, temperate zones
Wildlife: Bees, other pollinators
Care: Lift and divide to avoid congestion

◗ Grape hyacinth is a perennial from southern Europe, but it has come to feel at home in the UK. Undemanding and easy to grow, this common variety flowers in early spring and is a favourite among pollinators including bees and bumblebees. Its jewel-like colour is striking, and it looks especially good as a ground cover or underplanting, or when mixed with primroses and other spring bulbs. Plant 10cm (4in) deep in autumn.

Tulip
Tulipa 'Ballerina'

Sun: Full sun
Soil type: Chalk, loam, sand
Height: 60cm (24in)
Spread: 10cm (4in)
Hardiness: H6
Thrives: Grown worldwide, native of Europe, Asia and North Africa
Wildlife: Bees
Care: Once foliage has died, lift and store in a cool place

◗ This vibrant tangerine 'flame' tulip is a favourite for containers. It is 'lily flowered', which means its petals are elegantly long and thin with pointed ends and, as a bonus, it is scented. 'Ballerina' flowers in late spring and is striking in containers when paired with primroses or rising above a carpet of forget-me-nots. Plant in late autumn, 15–20cm (6–8in) deep.

Camassia
Camassia quamash

Sun: Full sun/partial shade
Soil type: All
Height: Up to 70cm (28in)
Spread: Up to 50cm (20in)
Hardiness: H5
Thrives: Temperate zones, native of northwestern US
Wildlife: Bees, other pollinators
Care: Mulch well in autumn to protect

This camassia is a great wildlife plant, loved by pollinators, which looks particularly good when planted in groups in meadow- or cottage-style potage containers. It has upright stems with clusters of starry nectar-rich flowers that mix well with grasses. It is originally from North America, where Native Americans ate them, roasted as a vegetable. Other varieties can be bought in white or lighter blue. Plant 8cm (3in) deep and 20cm (8in) apart.

Autumn crocus
Crocus sativus

Sun: Full sun
Soil type: All
Height: 15cm (6in)
Spread: 5cm (2in)
Hardiness: H6
Thrives: Europe, UK, central Asia, native of Greece
Wildlife: Bees, other pollinators
Care: Propagate by division

⬇ You don't expect to see a crocus in autumn, which makes this one all that more special. The honey-scented autumn crocus can get lost in a border at the end of the growing season, but it will shine if planted in a group near the edge of a container. Its prominent three-pronged red stigma are the source of saffron – pluck and dry it for colouring or flavouring. Plant the bulbs 10cm (4in) deep in late summer.

Round-headed leek
Allium sphaerocephalon

Sun: Full sun
Soil type: All
Height: 90cm (35in)
Spread: 10cm (4in)
Hardiness: H5
Thrives: Temperate zones, native of Sicily
Wildlife: Bees, butterflies, moths
Care: Can be lifted at end of season

Alliums are a boon to any planting plan, tall and majestic, with round heads that are magnets for bees and butterflies. This cultivar has egg-shaped flowerheads that start out green and turn maroon as it matures into early summer. They are held on slender stems that float among other plants. They look great as a clump or scattered among perennials. Plant 15cm (6in) deep and 15cm (6in) apart.

Plants to grow: Aquatic profiles

Aquatic plants bring a whole new dimension to container gardening, their flowers and foliage set off by the shimmer of the water surface. Even small water containers will attract masses of insects and butterflies. There is something extremely satisfying about sitting by your own small 'pond' while a dragonfly buzzes round, its iridescent wings catching the light on a sunny day.

STAR PLANT

Waterlily
Nymphaea alba

Sun: Full sun
Soil type: Chalk and sand, aquatic compost
Height: 10cm (4in)
Spread: Up to 1m (3ft)
Hardiness: H5
Thrives: Native of Europe and central Asia, introduced in New Zealand, China, Bangladesh
Wildlife: Bees, butterflies, hoverflies
Care: Regularly remove dying flowers and foliage

The UK native waterlily has large, flat, round leaves and upright teacup-shaped white flowers. For smaller containers, there is a wide variety of dwarf and miniature waterlilies. It flowers from late spring to early autumn and should be planted in a container with aquatic soil covered in pea shingle. It needs to be planted at the right depth from 75cm (30in) large to 15–20cm (6–8in) small. It doesn't like being splashed, loves a spring feed (via a feed ball in the soil) and benefits from regularly removing dying flowers and leaves. Every part is edible.

Marsh marigold
Caltha palustris

Sun: Full sun
Soil type: Sand
Height: 10-50cm (4-20in)
Spread: 50cm-1m (20-40in)
Hardiness: H7
Thrives: Northern hemisphere, temperate and subarctic zones
Wildlife: Bees, butterflies
Care: Cut back after flowering

● The UK native marsh marigold, with its nectar-rich bright yellow flowers in earliest spring, is a boon to early pollinators. It is a marginal plant, growing in moist boggy soil at the pond edge or in a planting basket placed just below the waterline. After flowering, it can be cut back (otherwise leaves can go grey). It may flower again later in the season. In a smaller container it will need to be divided in spring to avoid becoming too large.

Flowering rush
Butomus umbellatus

Sun: Full sun
Soil type: Chalk, sand, clay
Height: 60-90cm (24-35in)
Spread: 10-50cm (4-20in)
Hardiness: H5
Thrives: Temperate Eurasia, northern Africa, introduced in North America
Wildlife: Dragonflies, bees, butterflies
Care: Divide in spring

The flowering rush looks delicate with its slender green leaves and pink umbel flowers, but it is a hardworking multitasker. It provides height and summer colour and is a magnet for pollinators – especially dragonflies. Its flowers and tubers are edible. Plant just below the waterline up to 25cm (10in) deep in aquatic baskets and divide in spring.

Water forget-me-not
Myosotis scorpioides

Sun: Full sun/partial shade
Soil type: All
Height: 30cm (12in)
Spread: 50cm (20in)
Hardiness: H7
Thrives: North and South America, Europe, Asia and parts of Australia
Wildlife: Pollinators, amphibians
Care: Cut back after flowering

This UK native is easy to grow and a major draw for wildlife. It attracts bees, butterflies and other pollinators as well as amphibians – newts lay their eggs on the leaves in early spring. It has tiny blue flowers in late spring and early summer. Cut back after the first flowering and you may get more flowers in late summer.

Watercress
Nasturtium officinale

Sun: Full sun/partial shade
Soil type: Aquatic compost
Height: 10cm (4in)
Spread: Variable
Hardiness: H6
Thrives: Worldwide
Wildlife: Habitat for small aquatic creatures
Care: Cut back as necessary

⊕ Watercress, native to the UK, grows across the surface of a pond, so position on a shelf with its leaves just reaching the surface. It is fast-growing and is best suited to moving water, but also grows well in still water. The peppery leaves are packed with vitamin C, adding crunch and pizzazz to a wide variety of dishes, salads and soups. It has tiny white flowers in the summer. Watercress is an aquatic 'cut and come again' vegetable that also multitasks as a water filter and wildlife boon, providing shade for fish and other aquatic creatures.

Cotton grass
Eriophorum angustifolium

Sun: Sun/partial shade/full shade
Soil type: Aquatic compost
Height: 30cm (12in)
Spread: 50cm (20in)
Hardiness: H7
Thrives: Northern hemisphere
Wildlife: Habitat for insects
Care: Divide in spring

⊕ This UK native grass has long slender leaves that, in early and midsummer, are topped with white cottonwool 'flowerheads'. It thrives in both sun and shade and adds height as well as acts as a good backdrop for other smaller flowering aquatics. Unless it has been very cold, cotton grass will retain its leaves over winter, which gives it added year-round appeal. It can be grown submerged up to 15cm (6in) below the waterline or as a marginal in boggy conditions. It spreads via rhizomes and provides a good habitat for insects and other wildlife.

Plants to grow:
Dry garden plant profiles

Dry garden plants include alpines and succulents which, as they have so much in common, often find themselves sharing the same hypertufa trough or sink. Both prefer dry and sunny weather and well-draining soil. They are small and sturdy with a tendency to show off with their vibrantly coloured flowers that attract pollinators.

STAR PLANT

Lithodora
Lithodora diffusa 'Grace Ward'

Sun: Full sun
Soil type: Humus-rich, acidic
Height: 15cm (6in)
Spread: 15cm (6in)
Hardiness: H7
Thrives: Temperate zones, native of Mediterranean region
Wildlife: Bees
Care: Trim in autumn after flowering

⬅ This mat-forming evergreen perennial is an alpine star, providing eye-catching colour throughout spring and summer. Its small flowers are a startling sapphire blue, which contrasts well with its small, oblong, green leaves. It prefers acidic soil. Plant it in a pot filled with ericaceous compost and sink it under the soil line. It is native to southwestern Europe and its name aptly comes from the Greek lytho, which means 'stone', and dora, a 'gift'.

Houseleek

Sempervivum tectorum

Sun: Full sun
Soil type: Well drained, gritty
Height: 10cm (4in)
Spread: 30cm (12in)
Hardiness: H7
Thrives: Europe and North America, temperate zones
Wildlife: Bees
Care: Low maintenance

➲ The Romans believed the common houseleek would help protect your home from lightning strikes, while others thought it could ward off witches and bring good fortune and prosperity. For these reasons, it was often grown on house roofs (tectorum translates as 'roofs'). It is an evergreen, and is spread by offsets (thus the common name 'hens and chickens'). It looks especially good in a stone trough or hypertufa sink, with alpines and other succulents.

Thrift

Armeria maritima 'Splendens'

Sun: Full sun
Soil type: All
Height: 20cm (8in)
Spread: 20cm (8in)
Hardiness: H6
Thrives: Native of and widely grown in subarctic and temperate US zones
Wildlife: Bees, butterflies
Care: Deadhead

☚ Though sea thrift is found growing wild on cliffs and by the sea, it also works well in gardens and containers. It is a compact evergreen with bright deep-pink flowers in late spring and summer. The threepence coin (issued between 1937 and 1952) had a design of thrift on the reverse, perhaps a subtle way to emphasize its small-change thriftiness.

Siskiyou lewisia

Lewisia cotyledon

Sun: Full sun/partial shade
Soil type: All
Height: 30cm (12in)
Spread: 20cm (8in)
Hardiness: H6
Thrives: Cultivated widely, temperate zones, native of western US
Wildlife: Bees
Care: Low maintenance

This alpine is an evergreen perennial that forms rosettes of dark green leaves. In the spring and summer, it is topped by abundant funnel-shaped flowers that range in colour from magenta to pink to yellow, salmon and orange. Even individual petals may feature multiple colours. It's a showstopper that is also easy to grow and is drought tolerant once established.

Purple stonecrop

Sedum spathulifolium 'Purpureum'

Sun: Full sun/partial shade
Soil type: All
Height: 10cm (4in)
Spread: 30cm (12in)
Hardiness: H7
Thrives: Cultivated widely, native of western US
Wildlife: Bees
Care: Low maintenance

➔ Stonecrops are from dry and rocky locations and are drought tolerant. They are often used in alpine troughs and green roofs, and this variety – as an evergreen – provides year-round interest. It has a mound of purple-tinged fleshy leaves which, in late summer, are topped by starry yellow flowers that attract bees and other pollinators. Both this variety, and silvery 'Cape Blanco', are popular choices for containers.

Saxifraga

Saxifraga x *arendsii*

Sun: Full sun/partial shade
Soil type: Well drained, gritty
Height: 20cm (8in)
Spread: 10cm (4in)
Hardiness: H6
Thrives: Temperate and subalpine zones, cultivated worldwide
Wildlife: Bees
Care: Deadhead

There are many different types of saxifrage, also called 'rockfoil', which are small alpine and woodland plants. This hybrid is mat-forming (as are most) and has small white, pink or red flowers on short stems that rise above its green cushion leaves in late spring and early summer. It grows well in crevices or containers with very well-drained soil. Another popular Saxifraga is 'Winifred Bevington', with bright pink flowers and dark red stems.

Plants to grow: Herb profiles

Herbs are part of the 'incredible edible' group of plants.
They add soft colour, aroma and interest to any planting,
and they contribute flavour to many dishes. Most are excellent
companion plants for various fruit and vegetables and are
magnets for bees and insects. Many herbs are available in
varieties that add extra leaf and taste interest.

STAR PLANT

Thyme
Thymus vulgaris

Sun: Full sun
Soil type: Alkaline/neutral
Height: 10–15cm (4–6in)
Spread: 10–15cm (4–6in)
Hardiness: H5
Thrives: Northern hemisphere, Australia
Wildlife: Bees, generalist butterflies
such as skippers
Care: Cut back in spring

There is a wide spectrum of thyme varieties
with varying flower and leaf colours. The
leaves have a sharp earthy taste typically
used to flavour soups, stews, roasted meat, fish,
vegetables and savoury baking, and is also used
in teas and marinades. It is indigenous to the
Mediterranean region. Many varieties are
drought resistant, which makes it an ideal
plant to use in many countries' changing
climate. The wild variety *Thymus serpyllum*
is known as creeping thyme.

English marjoram
Origanum vulgare

Sun: Full sun/partial shade
Soil type: All
Height: 50cm–1m (20in–3ft)
Spread: 50cm–1m (20in–3ft)
Hardiness: H6
Thrives: Northern hemisphere, parts of Australia
Wildlife: Bees, butterflies
Care: Cut back in early spring

The UK native marjoram is the same species as oregano, the classic Mediterranean herb used in so many dishes. UK marjoram, grown in a cooler climate, has a slightly different scent, but the leaves still make an excellent kitchen seasoning. It is a food source for many types of insect and can be planted as part of a 'plants for pollinators' theme.

Borage
Borago officinalis

Sun: Full sun/partial shade
Soil type: All
Height: 50cm–1m (20in–3ft)
Spread: 50cm–1m (20in–3ft)
Hardiness: H5
Thrives: Europe, North and South America, parts of Asia, Australia, Africa
Wildlife: Bees
Care: Leave to self-seed after flowering

Borage, an annual, also known as starflower, grows bright blue flowers. Both the flowers and leaves have a cucumber flavour and can be used as a garnish, dried herb and in a variety of drinks. It is a companion plant for the vegetable garden, as it attracts bees and tiny wasps as well as repels certain critters that can affect tomatoes.

Dill
Anethum graveolens

Sun: Full sun
Soil type: All
Height: 50cm–1m (20in–3ft)
Spread: 50cm–1m (20in–3ft)
Hardiness: H4
Thrives: Temperate zones, grown worldwide
Wildlife: Bees
Care: Leave to self-seed after flowering

Dill weed – as it is sometimes known – is used as a herb in fish dishes and salads. In the past, it has been used as a remedy for coughs and headaches. Its feathery foliage and umbels of yellow flowers are attractive in cut-flower arrangements. Its flowers attract hoverflies and bees as well as butterflies, and caterpillars of the European swallowtail butterfly eat the leaves. It is used as a companion plant for asparagus, brassicas, cucumbers, lettuce and onion.

Fennel

Foeniculum vulgare

Sun: Full sun/partial shade
Soil type: All
Height: 1.5-2.5m (5-8ft)
Spread: 10-50cm (4-20in)
Hardiness: H5
Thrives: Widely grown across the world, native of Mediterranean region
Wildlife: Bees, other insects
Care: Drought resistant

Don't confuse the herb fennel with the vegetable Florence fennel, an annual grown for its bulbous white stalks. The herb, grown as a perennial, was probably introduced to the UK by the Romans and has now naturalized on verges and wasteland in some places. It is a statuesque elegant plant with feathery leaves and flat umbels of yellow flowers in the summer. Leaves and seeds have an aniseed-like taste and scent. The bronze varieties are particularly attractive in borders and containers.

Chives

Allium schoenoprasum

Sun: Full sun
Soil type: All
Height: 30cm (12in)
Spread: 30cm (12in)
Hardiness: H6
Thrives: Throughout northern hemisphere and other temperate zones
Wildlife: Bees
Care: Low maintenance

➲ The common chive, with its cheerful pompom pink-lavender flowers and thin cylindrical leaves, is a mainstay of every herb garden. Both leaves and flowers have a mild onion flavour. This is the ultimate 'cut and come again' plant, a versatile flavouring that perks up salads and soups and can be added to any number of dishes.

It can be grown as a potential deterrent for aphids, apple scab and mildew, and is a companion plant for carrots and tomatoes, among others.

Sage

Salvia officinalis

Sun: Full sun/partial shade
Soil type: Clay and loam
Height: 50cm-1m (20in-3ft)
Spread: 50cm-1m (20in-3ft)
Hardiness: H5
Thrives: Temperate zones, native of Europe
Wildlife: Bees
Care: Prune mid- to late spring

The Romans viewed sage as a sacred herb and used it in ceremonies and healing. It has pungent grey-green evergreen leaves and, in summer, short spikes of lavender flowers that are adored by bees. The earthy leaves are used in a variety of dishes, often with fatty meats – sage can be used mainly on its own and not with other herbs. It is extremely versatile, used to make teas, vinegars and butters, and is thought to aid digestion. It's said to be a good companion plant for brassicas.

Plants to grow: Climber profiles

Climbers give a container height and, when paired with an attractive plant support, can become a focal point or 'thriller' plant. They climb in three basic ways: twining, scrambling and clinging – and many become a kind of high-rise hotel for wildlife of all kinds.

STAR PLANT

Honeysuckle
Lonicera periclymenum

Sun: Full sun/partial shade
Soil type: All
Height: 4–8m (13–26ft)
Spread: Up to 4m (13ft)
Hardiness: H6
Thrives: Europe, parts of Australia and North America
Wildlife: Birds, bees, moths
Care: Trim back in late spring if needed

❂ This easy-to-grow native can often be seen in the wild, twining itself round hedgerows or in woodlands. It prefers light shade and has trumpet-like flowers, which vary in colour from light pink, yellow and cream. Its sweet scent is particularly noticeable at night, attracting pollinating moths. Honeysuckle has been called a 'wildlife hotel', as it attracts insects such as the elephant hawkmoth, which are then preyed upon by bats. It is also visited by birds, bees, lacewings and ladybirds.

Star jasmine
Trachelospermum jasminoides

Sun: Full sun/partial shade
Soil type: Loam, sand, clay
Height: 8-12m (26-39ft)
Spread: 4-8m (13-26ft)
Hardiness: H4
Thrives: Europe and parts of North America, Asia (native of China and Japan)
Wildlife: Bees
Care: Prune in spring if needed

⊕ This twining climber provides all-season interest – it has clusters of fragrant white flowers in the summer, while in winter, its evergreen leaves often develop bronze-red tints. It likes a sheltered warm spot and, in colder climates, will need winter protection. Provide a sturdy support, as it will need to be trained and cannot attach itself. Position it near a seating area for maximum scent appreciation.

Hops
Humulus lupulus 'Aureum'

Sun: Full sun/partial shade
Soil type: Chalk, loam, sand
Height: 4-8m (13-26ft)
Spread: 1.5-2m (5-7ft)
Hardiness: H6
Thrives: Europe and North America, parts of South America, Australia, Asia
Wildlife: Butterflies, moths, caterpillars
Care: Cut back in early winter

⊕ Hops are a common sight in the wild, twining their way through hedgerows. They have been cultivated to make beer for centuries. This cultivar has standout golden leaves (the sunnier the spot, the better the colour) and the female has aromatic cone-like flowers. Plant against a wall or fence or in large containers, over an arch or tepee. Hops attracts butterflies and moths and is a caterpillar food plant.

Sweet briar rose
Rosa rubiginosa

Sun: Full sun
Soil type: All
Height: 1.5-2.5m (5-8ft)
Spread: 1.5-2.5m (5-8ft)
Hardiness: H7
Thrives: Europe, North America, parts of South America, Australia, Africa
Wildlife: Bees, butterflies
Care: Prune in late winter

The UK native sweet briar rose can be pruned as a shrub or trained to climb up a tepee or other support. It has open, single, light pink flowers (apple scented) in the summer, followed by bright red fruit. The petals are edible and you can make jelly from the hips. It attracts bees, insects, birds, butterflies and moths, and is a caterpillar food plant. Sweet briar rose is a good 'backdrop' plant in a wildlife-friendly container that is set against a fence or wall.

Wild clematis or old man's beard
Clematis vitalba

Sun: Full sun/partial shade/full shade
Soil type: All
Height: 4-8m (13-26ft)
Spread: 4-8m (13-26ft)
Hardiness: H6
Thrives: Europe and western Asia, parts of North Africa, North America and Australia
Wildlife: Bees, hoverflies, birds
Care: Cut back in early spring

This scrambling climber, also known as Traveller's Joy, is the UK's only native clematis and is often seen in hedgerows, particularly in autumn, after its white flowers have turned into silky seedheads. Other than *Clematis heracleifolia* (which isn't a climber, but bushy) this is the only clematis to appear on the RHS Pollinators list.

For a more colourful cultivar, choose one with a simple petal structure that only climbs to 2.5m (8ft), such as the dark red Clematis 'Niobe' (EL) or the pink and white 'Carnaby'. Clematis likes to keep its roots cool, so you could underplant with some bee-friendly choices or apply a mulch.

Common ivy
Hedera helix

Sun: Partial/full shade
Soil type: All
Height: Variable
Spread: Variable
Hardiness: H6
Thrives: Europe and Australia, parts of North and South America
Wildlife: Bees, butterflies, moths, birds
Care: Prune in early spring

⊕ Ivy is a hero plant that can adapt to almost all gardening situations, including dry shade. It is an excellent climber but can also be used to 'trail' outside a container or as groundcover. It is a 'clinger', attaching itself via aerial roots on its stems to a support or wall. Dome-shaped flower clusters in autumn turn to dark purple/black fruit in winter. It is a food plant for some butterfly and moth larvae, and attracts birds, bees, hoverflies and wasps.

Plants to grow: Wild weed profiles

A 'weed' can be seen as a wild plant in the wrong place and, increasingly, one person's weed is being seen as another's wildlife magnet. Weeds are also unusually useful in other ways, including medicinally and as edibles. When used in containers, in a controlled fashion, they can look splendid and attract a plethora of bees and butterflies.

STAR PLANT

Common daisy
Bellis perennis

Sun: Full sun/partial shade
Soil type: All
Height: 10cm (4in)
Spread: 10cm (4in)
Hardiness: H7
Thrives: Worldwide
Wildlife: Bees
Care: Deadhead

The common daisy is seen as a turf weed, and a small industry has been devoted to finding ways to kill it. In general, the daisy seems to win and these days many people are setting aside areas of lawn where the daisy is left to flourish, ramping up the biodiversity factor. In colder climates its small flowers appear in late spring, but in warmer locations it can flower almost year-round. It is edible but has a bitter medicinal taste. It makes a cheerful and reliable container ground cover.

Cow parsley
Anthriscus sylvestris

Sun: Full sun/partial shade
Soil type: All
Height: Up to 1.5m (5ft)
Spread: 10–50cm (4–20in)
Hardiness: H7
Thrives: Widespread worldwide, native of UK, Europe, western Asia, northwest Africa
Wildlife: Bees, hoverflies, moths
Care: Divide if necessary

➲ Cow parsley, also known as wild chervil, transforms roadside verges into a sea of white in late spring, its large white umbels set off by green fern-like foliage. It is a member of the carrot family and the earliest to flower, a boon to bees and other insects as an early food source. It is also visited by certain moths and orange-tip butterflies. The dark-leaved variety, 'Ravenswing', works particularly well as a contrast plant in containers and is similarly attractive to wildlife.

Stinging nettle
Urtica dioica

Sun: Full sun/partial shade/full shade
Soil type: All
Height: Up to 1.5m (5ft)
Spread: 2.5–4m (8–13ft)
Hardiness: H7
Thrives: Most common in UK, Europe, North America, North Africa, Asia
Wildlife: Caterpillars, insects, birds
Care: Handle only with gloves; divide if necessary

➲ The common stinging nettle is ubiquitous in Britain and, when handled with care, is extremely useful. It is a great attractor of wildlife for caterpillars (of the small tortoiseshell and peacock butterflies) and ladybirds who love the aphids drawn to the plant. Nettles can be used medicinally, as a dye plant and to make plant fertilizer and garden twine, and it is edible. If planted in a container, make sure it doesn't get too close to passers-by.

White clover

Trifolium repens

Sun: Full sun
Soil type: All
Height: 10–50cm (4–20in)
Spread: 10–50cm (4–20in)
Hardiness: H7
Thrives: Worldwide, native of Europe, central Asia
Wildlife: Bumblebees, butterflies, mice
Care: Low maintenance

Clovers famously are trefoils with the occasional four-leaf find considered good luck. It is a 'green manure cover crop', which helps soil structure and fixes nitrogen. It is a great addition to compost heaps. Its flowers are edible and clover tea is commonly seen as helping some ailments. Woodmice collect the leaves, and bumblebees and some butterflies are attracted to the flowers. Red clover (*Trifolium pratense*) makes a particularly attractive container plant.

Dandelion

Taraxacum officinale

Sun: Full sun/partial shade
Soil type: All
Height: 15cm (6in)
Spread: 15m (50ft)
Hardiness: H7
Thrives: Temperate zones worldwide
Wildlife: Bees, butterflies, birds
Care: None

The common dandelion, reviled by lawn enthusiasts, is now being seen as a key plant for a wildlife garden. Its cheerful yellow flowers attract birds, bumblebees, butterflies, hoverflies, day-flying moths and solitary bees. Its fluffy seedhead clocks are the reason it spreads so easily, and its long taproot makes it particularly difficult to dig out. It's useful medicinally (diuretic) and is an edible that can be used to make 'coffee' and wine.

Teasel

Dipsacus fullonum

Sun: Full sun/partial shade
Soil type: All
Height: Up to 1m (3ft)
Spread: 50cm (20in)
Hardiness: H7
Thrives: Native of Eurasia, North Africa, introduced in the Americas, the rest of Africa, Australia
Wildlife: Bees, birds
Care: Low maintenance

Teasels are found on verges and wasteland; it is notable for seedheads that last all winter. It is a good architectural plant, with conical lilac flowers in the summer that attract bees and other pollinators. Its seedheads are striking and are a good food source for birds, especially goldfinches, which use their beaks to 'tease' out the seeds.

Charts and planners

When to plant

A container calendar of the ideal times for sowing seeds and planting trees and shrubs, flowers and grasses, aquatics and bulbs for all seasons.

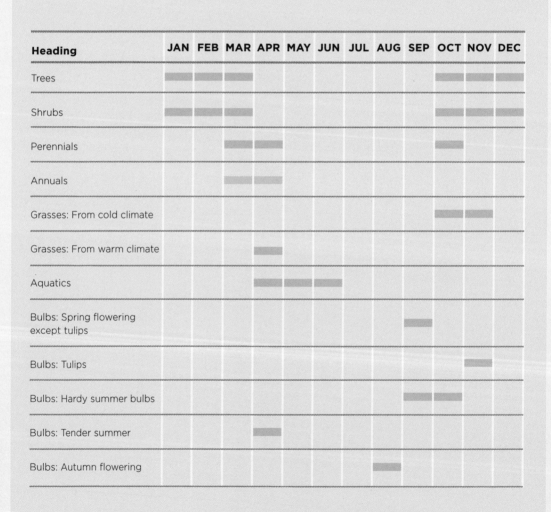

Planting and/or sowing from seed
Planting

Heading	JAN	FEB	MAR	APR	MAY	JUN	JUL	AUG	SEP	OCT	NOV	DEC
Trees	▬	▬	▬							▬	▬	▬
Shrubs	▬	▬	▬							▬	▬	▬
Perennials			▬	▬						▬		
Annuals			▬	▬								
Grasses: From cold climate										▬	▬	
Grasses: From warm climate				▬								
Aquatics				▬	▬	▬						
Bulbs: Spring flowering except tulips									▬			
Bulbs: Tulips											▬	
Bulbs: Hardy summer bulbs									▬	▬		
Bulbs: Tender summer				▬								
Bulbs: Autumn flowering								▬				

Bulbs planting depth

As a basic rule, bulbs in containers should be planted three times their depths, one bulb size apart. You can also use the chart below to plan a 'lasagne' pot, where layers of bulbs will provide a succession of different blooms for weeks on end. For instance, you could start with snowdrops, then daffodils, then tulips. The largest, which are also the later flowering bulbs, are planted deepest.

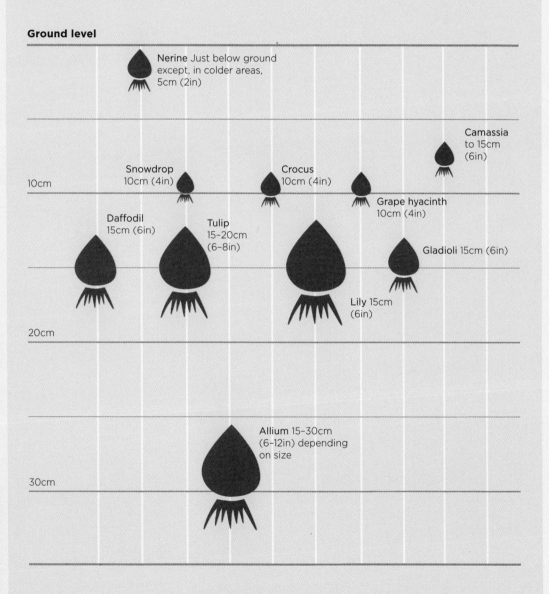

Ground level

Nerine Just below ground except, in colder areas, 5cm (2in)

Camassia to 15cm (6in)

Snowdrop 10cm (4in)

10cm

Crocus 10cm (4in)

Grape hyacinth 10cm (4in)

Daffodil 15cm (6in)

Tulip 15–20cm (6–8in)

Gladioli 15cm (6in)

Lily 15cm (6in)

20cm

Allium 15–30cm (6–12in) depending on size

30cm

Further reading

RHS Can I Grow Potatoes in Pots?
Sally Nex
Mitchell Beazley, 2022

The Climate Change Garden (Updated)
Sally Morgan & Kim Stoddart
Cool Springs Press, 2023

RHS Companion to Wildlife Gardening
Chris Baines
Frances Lincoln, 2016

The Crevice Garden
Kenton Seth & Paul Spriggs
Filbert Press, 2022

The Flower Yard
Arthur Parkinson
Kyle Books, 2021

The Garden Jungle
Dave Goulson
Vintage, 2020

RHS Gardening School
Simon Akeroyd & Ross Bayton
Mitchell Beazley, 2021

Grow Fruit and Vegetables in Pots
Aaron Bertelsen
Phaidon, 2020

RHS How to Grow the Low-carbon Way
Sally Nex
DK, 2021

RHS Resilient Gardening
Tom Massey
DK, 2023

RHS The Little Book of Small-space Gardening
Kay Maguire
Mitchell Beazley, 2018

Rewild Your Garden
Frances Tophill
Greenfinch, 2020

Wild About Weeds
Jack Wallington
Laurence King, 2019

Wild Food
Roger Phillips
Macmillan, 1983

WEB RESOURCES

Gardening Without Plastic
gardeningwithoutplastic.com

Royal Horticultural Society rhs.org.uk

The Wildlife Trusts wildlifetrusts.org.uk

The Woodland Trust woodlandtrust.org.uk

Royal Society for the Protection of Birds
rspb.org.uk

Index

A

aeonium 97
alkanet 111
allium 147, 169
alpines 18, 30, 60,
  62, 100–3, 152–5
  evergreen 153, 154
  hypertufa troughs
  17, 100
alyssum 101
anemone 139
angelica 111
annuals 24–5, 30,
  61, 62, 64, 71, 132–5
aphids 53, 61, 70,
  94, 120, 159, 166
apple 78–81, 93, 94,
  122
  crab 75, 90–1, 117
  stepover 81, 93, 95
  training 79, 81, 95
apricot 79
aquatic plants 30,
  106–9, 148–51
  edible 91, 151
aquilegia 77
arbours 15
arch supports 94
artichoke, globe 93,
  94
aspect 12–13, 63
aster 88, 105
alpine 101
astrantia 52
aubrieta 87, 101
aurinia 101

B

balance 65, 68
balconies 14, 32, 60,
  64

banana 96–7
bare-root plants 27,
  75
bats 71, 107, 161
bay 99, 127
beans 61
broad 121
  crimson 93
  ornamental value
  72
  runner 94
beech 77
bee hotel 89
bees 60, 70–1, 82,
  86–91, 95, 105, 109,
  110–11
beetroot 93
  interplanting 94
  rainbow 94
berries 70–1, 73, 99,
  125, 127
bindweed 111
birch 76, 91, 117
bird of paradise 97
birds 50, 60, 70–1,
  76, 82, 99, 106–7
blackberry 91, 93, 111
bluebell 76, 83, 87,
  88
blueberry 79, 80,
  123
blue fescue 142
bokashi bin 33
bone meal 48, 49
borage 61, 87, 88,
  91, 158
branch piles 36, 71,
  77, 111
brassicas 92
broccoli 94

brunnera 139
buddleja 87, 88, 111,
  126
bugle 105
bulbs 144–7
  lasagne planting
  145, 169
  planting depths
  169
burnet, wild 83, 84,
  91
buttercup 111
butterflies 60, 70–1,
  84,
  86–91, 95, 110–11
buying plants 25,
  27, 69

C

cabbage 75, 92, 93
cabbage white
  butterfly 92
caddisfly 107
Caladium 97
Calamagrostis 105
camassia 147, 169
campanula 101
campion, red 83
canna 97
caraway 88
carbon capture 61,
  70,
  72, 77
carbon footprint 19,
  34,
  70, 72
cardoon 75, 93
carex 99, 105
carrot, wild 83, 84
carrot fly 94

caterpillars 76, 89,
  94, 116, 117, 120, 143,
  158, 162, 163, 166
catkins 76, 115, 117
celandine 111
chamomile 83
chard 93
  rainbow 94, 95,
  119
chasmophytes 101
cherry 79, 80, 95
chervil, wild 91, 166
chives 75, 88, 93,
  94, 159
  companion plant,
  as a 94
cleaning containers
  29, 52
clematis 36, 163
climbing plants 15,
  69, 70
  evergreen 99, 162
  plant profiles
  160–3
  potagers 94–5
clover 91, 111, 167
coleus 97
colour 61, 68
comfrey tea 46, 48,
  49, 90, 93
companion plants
  52, 60, 70, 135
  herbs 157–9
  potagers 61, 92,
  93, 94
compost see potting
  compost
composting 32–5
conifers 99
corn cockle 83

cornflower 24, 83, 84, 93, 94, 133
cornus 75, 76, 105
cosmos 83, 84, 87, 88, 135
cottage gardens 62
cotton grass 107, 151
courgette 61
courtyard gardens 78
cow parsley 111, 166
cowslip 83
crazy containers 96-7
crevice gardens 100-3
crocks 29, 35, 97
crocosmia 105
crocus 99, 102, 169
    autumn 147
crowfoot 107
curry plant 99
cuttings, propagation by 26
cyclamen 99, 101, 102

D
daffodil 169
dahlia 38, 97, 131
daisy 51, 87, 88, 105, 111, 165
damselflies 70, 107
dandelion 51, 70, 91, 110-11, 167
deadnettle 111
deer 50, 139, 142
delosperma 101
Deschampsia 105, 141
design
    considerations 62-8
    planting plan 66-9
dill 75, 93, 158

companion plant, as a 158
diseases 52
division, propagation by 26
dock 111
dormice 115, 116
dragonflies 60, 70, 72, 91, 107, 109
drainage 29, 34, 35, 41
    rain gardens 104
drought resistance 41, 129, 157
dry crevice gardens 100-3, 152-5
dusty miller 62, 99

E
east-facing sites 13
echinacea 93, 94, 105
edelweiss 101
edibles 70, 72, 109
    aquatic plants 91, 151
    ornamental 118-23, 134
    wild 90-1
elderflower 74, 75, 76, 90-1, 105, 125
equipment 20-1
espaliers 79, 81, 95
euphorbia 105
evening primrose 87, 89
evergreens 62, 97, 98-9, 135, 155
    alpines 153, 154
    climbing plants 99, 162
    ferns 77, 137, 159
    grasses 141, 143
    herbs 75, 93, 127
    semi-evergreens 138, 141, 143

succulents 154
topiary 98-9
exposure 12, 14, 63

F
fabric containers 19
Fatsia japonica 97
feather grass 141
fennel 75, 84, 87, 88, 91, 93, 159
    bronze 94
ferns 63, 76-7, 99, 139
    evergreen 77, 137, 159
fertilizers/feeding 46-9, 107
fish, blood and bone 48, 49
foliage 61
forest bathing 74
forget-me-not 146
    water 107, 150
formal gardens 62, 98-9
fountain grass 99
foxes 15, 117
frogs 70-1, 72, 106-9
frost 46, 54, 99, 114
frost-proof
    containers 17, 99
fruit 30, 72
    feeding 47
    orchards 78-81
    ornamental 120, 122-3
    pollination 79
    potagers 92-5
    stepover 81, 93, 95
    trained trees 79, 81, 95
    wild edibles 90-1
fuchsia 97
fungal diseases 40

G
garlic mustard 51, 111
geranium 105, 111
ginger lily 97
gladioli 169
gloves 21
gooseberry 79, 80
grape 79
grape hyacinth 87, 88, 146, 169
grasses 77, 99, 104-5, 107-9, 141
grit 26, 30, 34
ground cover 51, 75, 93, 111, 163
grouping plants 58-61
growing medium *see potting compost*

H
hanging containers 15, 19
hardiness scale 114
hard shield fern 137
hart's tongue fern 139
hawthorn 73, 75, 76-7, 91, 99, 116
hazel 36, 75, 76-7, 115
heather, winter 99
helenium 131
hellebore 99, 138
herbicides 107
herb robert 111
herbs 30, 41, 75, 88, 90
    companion plants, as 92, 157-9
    evergreen 75, 93, 127
    plant profiles 156-9
    potagers 92-5
    wild 91

hogweed 111
holly 62, 98–9
hollyhock 93
honesty 83, 93
honeysuckle 88, 89, 161
  winter 99
hoof and horn 48, 49
hop 162
hornwort 107, 109
horsetail 107
hosepipes 41
hosta 63, 138
houseleek 101, 103, 154
hoverflies 86–9, 109
hügelkultur 35
humidity 60, 61
hydrangea 105, 127
hypertufa troughs 17, 100
hyssop 88
  anise hyssop 91

I
Ilex 99
insulating
  containers 19
intermediate bulk
  containers 18, 76
  interplanting 94
  pocket forests 75
  potagers 94
iris 105, 107
irrigation systems 43
ivy 36, 60, 70, 73, 87, 99, 163

J
Japanese forest
  grass 142
jasmine 89
  star 162
  winter 99
juniper 99

K
kale 75, 93, 94
  black 93, 94, 120
knapweed 83, 111
kneeling pad 21

L
'lasagne' bulb
  planting 145, 169
lavender 62, 87, 93, 130
layers and levels 65, 68, 74–5
leek
  companion plant,
    as a 94
Lenten rose 138
lettuce 93, 94, 95, 121
  interplanting 94
lewisia 155
lichens 77
lily 169
liquorice mint 91
Lithodora 153
lungwort 87

M
mallow 87
manure 34
maple, paperbark 116
marigold 24, 61, 88, 93, 135
  companion plant,
    as a 94, 135
  French 87
  marjoram 83, 84, 87, 88, 91, 158
  wild 111
marsh marigold 107, 150
May tree 116
meadow plantings 68, 82–5
meadowsweet 111

Mediterranean
  plantings 63
medlar 80
metal containers 19
Michaelmas daisy 87
microclimates 59, 61, 70
  crevice gardens 101
milfoil 107
mint 91
  water 72, 91, 109
mirrors 14
Miscanthus 105
Miyawaki, Akira 74
mosses 77
moths 76, 86–9, 115, 116, 117, 122, 125, 126, 135, 147, 161–3, 166, 167
mulch 34, 35, 41, 51
mullein 111

N
nasturtium 24, 75, 91, 93, 134
  companion plant,
    as a 94, 120
nectarine 79
nectar plantings 62, 70, 86–9, 102
nematodes 53
nepeta 93
  companion plant,
    as a 94
nerine 169
netting 36, 50
nettle 70, 73, 89, 110–11, 166
  nettle tea 48, 49
newts 107
Nicotiana 62
night-scented plants 87, 89

night-scented stock 89
nitrogen 47
north-facing sites 13
nutrients 47

O
oak 77
old man's beard 163
onion
  companion plant,
    as a 94
  seedheads 95
oregano 158
organic fertilizers 46–9
Oudolf, Piet 62
overcrowding 34
ox-eye daisy 83

P
palm
  fan 97
  windmill 97
pansy 99
paperbark maple 116
parsley 75, 93, 94
peach 79
pear 78–81, 93
  stepover 81, 93, 95
peas 93
peat 25, 27, 28, 31
perennials 24, 26–7, 30, 61, 128–31
perlite 26, 31, 34, 100
permanent plantings 77
pesticides 46, 52, 71
pests 52–3, 60, 107, 108
  companion plants
    see companion plants

pheasant's tail grass
99, 141
Phlox subulata 101
phosphates 47
picea 99
pickerelweed 107,
109
pine 99
pineapple 97
pink 101
plantain, water 107
plastic 16, 18, 27, 36,
75
plug plants 25, 85
plum 79, 93, 122
pollinating insects
59, 60-1, 69, 70-1,
80, 86-9
pollination 80
pollution screens
59, 70
pomegranate 80
ponds 70-1, 72-3,
106-9
poppy 24, 83, 84,
93, 94
California 83
Oriental 26
porches 14
potagers 92-5
colour 93, 94-5
companion plants
61, 92, 93, 94,
135, 158
interplanting 94
seedheads 95
potassium 47, 48
pot-bound plants
26, 27
pot feet 99
potting compost
25, 26-7
aeration 26
aquatic plants 30
for cuttings 26

drainage 29, 34,
35, 41
making 28, 29,
32-3
peat-free 31
replacing 34-5
water retentive
31, 41
potting up 35
prairie plantings 62,
68
prickly heath 99
primrose 87, 88, 93,
146
privet 98-9
propagation 26-7

Q
quaking grass 141
quince 79, 80, 123

R
rabbits 50, 123, 139
radish 93, 94
seedheads 95
ragweed 111
rain 14
harvesting 14, 25,
40-2
rain gardens 104-5
rain shadow 14
raspberry 91
recycled containers
16-17, 19
redcurrant 95
repetition 65, 68
rhizosphere 101
rockfoil 101
roots
crevice gardens
101
feeding 47
pot-bound plants
26, 27
root cuttings 26
shallow 41

rose 93, 105
rosehips 91, 99
sweetbriar 91, 163
wild/dog 75, 91,
94, 99, 111
rosemary 63, 75, 91,
92, 93, 94, 99, 105,
127
round-headed leek
147
rowan 75, 117
rudbeckia 88, 105
rush 91, 107-9
flowering 150

S
sacrifice crops 120
sage 75, 77, 92, 93,
99, 159,
salvia 87, 129, 159
sand 26, 30, 34
saucers and reservoirs
16, 41, 43
Saxatiles 101
saxifrage 101, 155
scabious, field 83,
84
scale insects 53
scorching 40, 44
screen plantings 14,
60
sea buckthorn 91
sea holly 87
seasonal checklist
54-5
sea thrift 101
seaweed 48, 49, 93
sedges 105
sedum 73
seed, growing from
25, 27, 30
growing medium
30
seed pots 25
seedheads 60, 70,
84-5, 134, 167

grasses 141, 143
vegetable
potagers 95
sempervivum 101,
154
shade 12-13, 60, 63,
72
shade lover profiles
136-9
shrubs *see trees and
shrubs*
Siberian bugloss
139
silver fern 99
siting containers
12-15
potager pots 92
size, container 16,
17, 59, 63, 67
size, plant 27, 68
skimmia 99
slugs 40, 52, 107,
108, 119, 121, 138
smoke bush 126
snails 40, 52, 107,
108, 138
sneezeweed 131
snowdrop 99, 169
soil improvers 32,
34
sorbus 76
sorrel 91
sound 104
south-facing sites
13
space 64
squash 93
squirrels 50
starflower 131
stone containers 16,
19, 100-3
stonecrop 101, 155
strawberry 61, 72,
93, 120
wild 91

succession planting 68

succulents 30, 41, 62, 100–3, 152–5

sunflower 24, 73, 83, 87, 88, 93, 94, 134

sunlight 12–13, 63

supports 36–9, 68, 88, 94

sustainable drainage system 104–5

sweet cicely 91

sweetcorn 75, 93, 94

sweet pea 24, 93, 94

sweet rocket 87, 88

T

teasel 51, 73, 111, 167

temperature regulation 15, 70

tepee supports 36, 39, 65, 68, 94

terracotta 16, 17, 29

thistle 51, 93

thrift 154

thyme 63, 75, 87, 88, 91, 92, 93, 157

creeping 101

toads 106

tobacco plant 87, 89, 135

tomato, cherry 121

tools 20–1, 52

sharpening 20

top-dressing 34

topiary 62, 98–9

trailing plants 65, 120, 163

traveller's joy 163

tree fern 97

trees and shrubs 14, 59, 61, 63, 65, 70, 72

evergreen 98–9

fruit 78–81, 91, 92–5

pocket forests 74–7

shrub profiles 122–7

topiary 98–9

trained 79, 81, 95

tree profiles 115–17

wild edibles 90–1

tropical plants 62, 96–7

tulip 102, 146, 169

twine 21, 36

V

vegetables 30, 49, 92–5

interplanting 94

ornamental 93, 94–5, 119–21

potagers 92–5

root 45

Verbascum 26

Verbena bonariensis 87

vermiculite 34

vertical space 64, 65, 67, 68

vervain 131

vetch 111

vine weevil 53

W

wallflower 87

walls 12, 14, 15, 19, 78

fruit trees trained against 79, 81, 95

living 19

water butts 14, 40, 42

watercress 72, 91, 107, 109, 151

watering 14, 40–5

container size and 16

crevice gardens 103

harvesting rainwater 14, 25, 40–2

overwatering 40, 46

saucers and reservoirs 16, 41, 43

self-watering methods 43–5

watering cans 21, 40

waterlily 91, 106–9

water retentive compost 31, 41

water skaters 109

water striders 107

wavy hair grass 141

weeds 41, 45, 50–1, 70, 84, 110–11

weed profiles 164–7

west-facing sites 13

wicking beds 43–5

wildflowers 30, 46, 73, 77, 82–5

wildlife 15, 16, 17, 36, 50, 60–1, 104

attracting 70–3, 86–9, 95, 106–11

wildlife maps 68

wildlife surveys 71

willow 36

willowherb 111

wind 14, 92

windflower 139

windowsills 14, 25

winter 98–9

wooden containers 16, 18

potagers 94–5

wormeries 48, 49

Y

yarrow 130

yew 98–9

PICTURE CREDITS

Guide: TL Top left, ML Middle left BL Bottom left, TR Top right, MR Middle Right BR Bottom right

2 Lois GoBe/Shutterstock, 5 GAP Photos/Nicola Stocken, 6-7 ParinPix/Shutterstock, 8-9 GAP Photos/Nicola Stocken, 10-11 RHS / Sarah Cuttle, 12 RHS / Tim Sandall, 13 itakefotos4u/Shutterstock, 13 TR Makhnach_S/Shutterstock, 14 left Dulyanut Swdp/Getty Images, 14 right Groomee/Getty Images, 15 Kostikova Natalia/Shutterstock, 16 nieriss/Shutterstock, 17 top Dagmar Breu/Shutterstock, 17 middle Geo-grafika/Getty Images, 17 bottom J M Photography/Shutterstock, 18 TL GAP Photos/Nicola Stocken - The IBC Pocket Forest. Designer: Sara Edwards, 18 ML Oxana Medvedeva/iStockphoto, 18 ML & BL GAP Photos/Nicola Stocken, 18 TR Bond JP/Shutterstock, 19 TL Galina Grebenyuk/Shutterstock, 19 TR Ellen Rooney / Alamy Stock Photo, 19 MR Renata Ty/Shutterstock, 19 BR Antony-Kemp/iStockphoto, 22-23 GAP Photos, 24 GAP Photos/Carole Drake - Garden: Am Brook Medow, Devon; Owners: Jennie and Jethro Marles, 25 Gheorghe Mindru/Shutterstock, 26 Top GAP Photos/Paul Debois, 26 Bottom left to right Wilfred Huddlestone/Shutterstock, Peerawong Wattana/Shutterstock, Graham Corney/Shutterstock, 27 TanyaJoy/Shutterstock, 28 GAP Photos/Mark Bolton, 30 All Pixel-Shot/Shutterstock, 31 AndreaObzerova/iStockphoto, 32 Kaca Skokanova/Shutterstock, 33 MyBears/Shutterstock, 34 GAP Photos/Hanneke Reijbroek, 35 & 37 GAP Photos, 40 Peter Klausmann/Shutterstock, 41 Imgorthand/Getty Images, 42 GAP Photos/Jacqui Hurst - Designer: Martyn Wilson, 43 RaffMaster/Shutterstock, 47 TR walkerone/Shutterstock, 47 BL agrophoto/Shutterstock, 47 BR GAP Photos/Claire Higgins, 48 GAP Photos, 49 left Foxxy63/Shutterstock, 49 right Ashley-Belle Burns/Shutterstock, 50 blightylad-infocus/iStockphoto, 51 TL nadia_if/Shutterstock, 51 ML Kevin White Photographer/Shutterstock, 51 ML Andi111/Shutterstock, 51 BL Mr. Meijer/Shutterstock, 51 TR grafxart/Shutterstock, 52 Tom Meaker/Shutterstock, 53 Ballygally View Images/Shutterstock, 53 TR Young Swee Ming/Shutterstock, 53 MR F.Neidl/Shutterstock, 53 BR Lutsenko_Oleksandr/Shutterstock, 54 left GAP Photos, 54 right lcrms/Shutterstock, 55 left Yuriy Bogatirev/Shutterstock, 55 right GAP Photos/Robert Mabic, 56-57 GAP Photos/Marion Brenner, 58 GAP Photos/Nicola Stocken, 59 top GAP Photos/Richard Bloom - by Alan Gray at East Ruston Old Vicarage gardens, Norfolk, UK, 59 middle Peter Carruthers/iStockphoto, 59 bottom GAP Photos/Graham Strong, 60 top Ingrid Balabanova/Shutterstock, 60 middle GAP Photos/Andrea Jones - Design: Joe Swift, 60 bottom joppo/Shutterstock, 61 left Lois GoBe/Shutterstock, 61 right Nabiha Dahhan / Westend61 GmbH / Alamy Stock Photo, 62 aimintang/iStockphoto, 63 left Tannjuska, 63 right GAP Photos/Elke Borkowski, 64 Patsy Davies / Alamy Stock Photo, 65 GAP Photos/Heather Edwards - Design: Ellie Edkins, 66 andreaskrappweis/Getty Images, 71 Erni/Shutterstock, 72 La Rose/Shutterstock, 73 top GAP Photos/J S Sira - Design: David and Harry Rich - Sponsor: Bord Na Mona UK, 73 bottom Martin FowlerShutterstock, 75 GAP Photos/Matt Anker, 78 Ninellles/Shutterstock, 79 Derek Harris / Alamy Stock Photo, 82 GAP Photos/Graham Strong, 83 ArchivalSurvival / Alamy Stock Photo, 87 TL aniana/Shutterstock, 87 ML Craig Russell/Shutterstock, 87 ML GAP Photos/Jonathan Buckley, 87 BL Fenneke Smouter/Shutterstock, 87 TR MarinaGreen/Shutterstock, 90 GAP Photos/Sarah Cuttle - Designer: Stephen Hall, 91 top GAP Photos, 91 bottom GAP Photos/Gary Smith, 92 GAP Photos/Heather Edwards - Design: Philippa Pearson, 93 GAP Photos/Andrea Jones, 96 MaCross-Photography/Shutterstock, 97 GAP Photos/Julia Boulton, 98 Joanna Kossak/ RHS, 99 Magdalena Sinakova/Shutterstock, 100 GAP Photos/Carole Drake, 101 Wiert nieuman/Shutterstock, 104 Anton Dios/Shutterstock, 105 GAP Photos/Mark Turner, 106 Susan Edmondson/Shutterstock, 107 Nigel Noyes / Alamy Stock Photo, 110 garfotos / Alamy Stock Photo, 111 left GAP Photos, 111 right GAP Photos/Jonathan Buckley, 112-113 & 114 GAP Photos/Fiona Lea, 115 Przemyslaw Muszynski/Shutterstock, 116 left tatianaput/Shutterstock, 116 right blickwinkel/McPHOTO/HRM/Alamy Stock Photo, 117 Sahara Prince/Shutterstock 118 Nyura/Shutterstock, 119 RobynCharnley/Shutterstock, 120 left V_Sot_Visual_Content/Shutterstock, 120 right lenic/Shutterstock, 121 U106215, CC BY-SA 4.0 <https://creativecommons.org/licenses/by-sa/4.0>, via Wikimedia Commons, 122 left Stuarts Photography/Shutterstock, 122 right LFM Visuals/Shutterstock, 123 left Valentyn Volkov/Shutterstock, 123 right nnattalli/Shutterstock, 124 GAP Photos/Christa Brand, 125 Diana Taliun/Shutterstock, 126 left H Athey/Shutterstock, 126 right Foxxy63/Shutterstock, 127 Roxana Bashyrova/Shutterstock, 128 gollykim/istock, 129 guentermanaus/Shutterstock, 130 left lenic/Shutterstock, 130 right delobol/Shutterstock, 131 Kyle Bagley/Shutterstock, 132 RHS/Tim Sandall, 133 Badon Hill Studio/Shutterstock, 134 left Rafael SANTOS RODRIGUEZ/Shutterstock, 134 right gollykim/iStockphoto, 135 Steve Taylor ARPS / Alamy Stock Photo, 136 & 137 Ian Grainger/Shutterstock, 138 top RM Floral / Alamy Stock Photo, 138 bottom GAP Photos/Christa Brand, 139 Nancy J. Ondra/Shutterstock, 140 Molly Shannon/Shutterstock, 141 Beekeepx/Shutterstock, 142 top Martina Unbehauen/Shutterstock, 142 bottom Molly Shannon/Shutterstock, 143 Kimmo Keskinen/Shutterstock, 144 RHS/Neil Hepworth, 145 CBCK-Christine/Getty Images, 146 top Peter Turner Photography/Shutterstock, 146 bottom Ian Grainger/Shutterstock, 147 Esin Deniz/Shutterstock, 148 Pietro Tasca/Shutterstock, 149 IvanaStevanoski/Shutterstock, 150 Gertjan Hooijer/Shutterstock, 151 left tamu1500/Shutterstock, 151 right Leonid Ikan/Shutterstock, 152 GAP Photos/Nicola Stocken, 153 Ian Grainger/Shutterstock, 154 top WR7/Shutterstock, 154 bottom raymond orton/Shutterstock, 155 Mike Russell/Shutterstock, 156 RHS/Sarah Cuttle, 157 Olga Miltsova/Shutterstock, 158 andy lane / Alamy Stock Photo, 159 DragonWen/Shutterstock, 160 NATTANAN KLOENPRATHOM/Shutterstock, 161 Flegere/Shutterstock, 162 left Konstantinos Livadas/Shutterstock, 162 right Belikart/Shutterstock, 163 Marie Shark/Shutterstock, 164 Jacky Parker Photography/Getty Images, 165 Cristina Ionescu/Shutterstock, 166 bottom Bits And Splits/Shutterstock, 166 top GroundedTwenty7/Shutterstock, 167 Sandra Standbridge/Shutterstock

Every effort has been made to credit the copyright holders of the images used in these books. We apologise for any unintentional omissions or errors and will insert the appropriate acknowledgements to any companies or individuals in subsequent editions of the work.

PICTURE CREDITS